THE AUTHOR'S ON-LINE PRESENCE COMPANION HANDBOOK

HOW TO FIND READERS

BARB DROZDOWICH

ISBN: 978-1-988821-18-4

❋ Created with Vellum

DEDICATION

This is dedicated to all writers who are great storytellers, but struggle with the technology side of writing and publishing a book.

NOTE OF THANKS

I would like to thank you for buying one of my books!

I tend to focus on the technical tasks that authors and bloggers need to learn. As of this publishing I have 17 books in print and several more in various stages of completion. I'm always looking to be helpful - often creating books around subjects that I get a lot of questions on from authors and bloggers just like you.

At the end of this book is the link join my group of readers and get some free help with the technical subjects.

On to the book - I hope you enjoy and learn lots!

CONTENTS

PREFACE

Welcome to the 1st edition of this book as a handbook and welcome to the ever-changing world of today's author. My name is Barb Drozdowich and I work as a blog designer and technical trainer. In my work, I focus primarily on authors. In fact, I've meet with and talked to a wide variety of authors across the spectrum of experience during my years of work. Because of this I see the trouble spots. Over the last 5+ years I have created 17 books that help explain various subjects to authors – usually at a beginner level and usually because of a 'pain point' or point of confusion that I see in my work. I assume that if I see 10 authors who all have the same questions, there are a lot more that I don't talk to with the same concerns.

Because of my background in technical training I have a lot of experience breaking complicated subjects down into more simple, easy to manage sections. I use every day language and leave the technobabble for chatting with my geeky friends. I approach each book from the beginner level. Many of my books move from a beginner to what I would consider an intermediate level, but I never start explaining a subject at a level that is too difficult for most beginners.

I think it's important to realize that you are not alone in your need to learn a lot of things. Almost all authors start out at the same basic point – they have written a really good story but struggle with how to proceed from that point. The learning curve for publishing is steep – whether technical subjects are your forte or not, there is a lot to learn in order to publish and sell books. I do believe that this mass of learning is doable and I have a lot of authors I work with that have done just that.

In the author world there are a lot of folks who claim they don't need an "Author Platform." They don't see the point and in many cases don't really understand what they are saying 'No' to. Because of this, I've decided to change the name of this edition and add some more up to date information with respect to targeting readers. As you can see from the front cover, the title is now *The Author's On-Line Presence*. While I found that many authors are intimidated by the title of Author Platform, many can relate to the term On-Line Presence. As authors, our focus is on communicating in various ways with readers. More on this as we go along.

Let's create an analogy: You have moved to a new city, you have a couple of kids and you need to create a new community for yourself. You need to find friends, you need to meet the neighbours, you need to find schools for your kids, sports/arts activities for your kids – at a most basic point, you need to find a grocery store. Part of your new community will be connections with people and part will be your environment. You will chat with your neighbours, join a fitness club or join a book club. You will chat with other parents while waiting for school to go in or get out if your kids are young and likely you will chat with other parents while you kids are doing their various activities. If you work outside of the house, you will learn whom the go-to person is in your company to fix your computer, fix your pay cheque or order you some more pens. You will find somewhere to buy/eat lunch.

What I've described above is no different in the author world. We need to find like-minded people who will help us with, or commiserate with us, in our publishing journey. We need to find and chat with readers of our books.

In this day and age, we either "Google" things, or we ask for recommendations. Many readers in today's world get to the end of a great book and look for more information on the author – they look for more of the author's books to read or they try to learn more about the author. Readers will do that searching in "their" worlds. Perhaps their first action is to "Google" the author, perhaps they head to Amazon to find what else the author has written or perhaps they search for information on Facebook. Whatever readers do, we need to make sure they find some information in their searches. We want to be helpful – we want readers to be successful in their searching, not be disappointed and wander off to learn about a different author. We want readers to learn more about us and our books, and perhaps to purchase a book, subscribe to a blog, join a newsletter – whatever they choose in their mission to learn more.

Now that I've given you reason to learn more about this topic, let's jump into the subject of this book. This version of "The Author's On-Line Presence" is the handbook version. I've had authors asking me for this for a couple of years - authors who want to jot down some thoughts as they progress through the content. The content is the same as the regular paperback version of this book, but I've added in some lines to collect your thoughts at the end of each chapter as well as space to answer questions or brainstorm about various questions that come up in the content.

Without further ado...let's move on to learning about an author's on-line presence!

INTRODUCTION

Welcome to the subject of The Author's Platform – or as I prefer to call it – The Author's On-line Presence. This "platform" or "presence" can be described in various ways – as the launch site for all marketing activities, as the place readers can find authors & learn more, and as the place that allows the author to chat with and network with readers from every country in the world.

My name is Barb Drozdowich and I'm a voracious reader – and that's where my world intersected with the author world. I entered the publishing world as a book blogger on *Sugarbeat's Books*, bringing with me a master's degree in education and several decades of experience in teaching and technical training. The technical aspect of the author world interested me right from the start. I have spent years explaining technical subjects to non-technical people – at the college and university level as well as the corporate world of banking as a technical trainer. The world of blogs and social media is a world that I understand and I'm comfortable in. The manual you're now reading was born through my involvement helping many authors just like you navigate the quickly changing publishing world.

My first book was published in early 2013 in response to concerns raised by authors I worked with. I help a lot of authors understand the publishing world one-on-one, but by sharing my knowledge in a book, I can help a lot more people. I come at the publishing world with a different view-point than many authors. I'm not an author who has managed to learn things that I want to share. I'm a technical trainer, who has many years of experience explaining technical subjects. I also understand the 'big picture' of why we do what we do. I may explain subjects at a beginner level but my technical background and education has me understanding exactly why I suggest various things. I'm not just following other people's suggestions, or explaining "what worked for me," I'm taking my big picture understanding and simplifying it for beginners and non-technical people to understand.

This is my way of saying that although on the surface, building an on-line presence may seem daunting, I will explain the basics in this book in a non-technical, easy-to-understand way.

LET's get back to the topic of what an author's on-line presence (or as many call it, author platform) is. Many authors understand the 'in person' activities of being an author. They have gone to book-signings, readings, conferences, etc. This, for many, is a comfortable world – one that is understood by most authors. The on-line world...not so much. In today's global economy, an author's readers may live in any country. In fact, by allowing Amazon or iTunes or Kobo to sell your books, they will be available in every country in the world. They may be read in paperback form, but more likely for many authors, they will be read on an e-reader, a Kindle, a tablet or even a phone. All that is needed is a connection to the Internet and readers can be purchasing books at their convenience.

HUNDREDS OF STUDIES tell us that book buying is a relationship activity. Many people put more thought into buying a book than they do their morning coffee. Today's readers want to develop a relationship with authors. The want to do more than buy a book – they want to learn about the author. Since the Internet has brought the world to your doorstep, the process of chatting with readers may prove easier than you think.

The question of the day: "Do authors need an online presence or an author platform?" I believe they do. Many books have been written on the subject of selling books. Bookshelves, both physical and virtual, are littered with different points of view. Everyone claims they can help you sell a million copies. Everyone claims to have an "Easy" button. But do they?

What books do you know that have sold a million copies? Are they all examples of great literature? Are the authors in line to win a Pulitzer Prize? No? Then why does a particular book sell so many copies? In many cases, the book simply catches a wave of attention.

Name a book that is hugely popular and you've found a book built on relationships. Think about it: the majority of the time, we buy books based on a suggestion from a friend or another trusted source, or we purchase due to word-of-mouth praise or media publicity. You either wanted to see what all the fuss was about or considered reading it to see if it was really that bad!

If you are an indie author, or simply a new author, you need to create buzz about your book. I often refer to the creation and marketing tasks as "Operation Book." Just think of Operation Book as a strategy game—the authors who learn to play this game the best will sell the highest number of books. Is it really that simple? It can be.

Once you understand the rules, you will play the game like a master. Operation Book works differently for different types of books. However, each book requires:

• Readers
• Fans

• Methods of communication

You'll notice I didn't mention great cover art, flawless formatting, the absence of spelling mistakes or other mandatory elements of good publishing. Miss any of these elements and it can count as points against you in Operation Book. But we all know of books that have these issues yet still sell lots of copies. For our purposes, we'll focus on how to use the author platform as a method of marketing and communication or, in other words, Operation Book.

BEFORE WE GO ANY FURTHER, if you are looking for an "Easy" button, you won't find one here. Can all the information in this book be found in on-line articles – blog posts and the like? Yes, but the reason for putting this book together, beyond being helpful, is to share **correct** information. There is a lot of incorrect information available online. All of the information in this book is researched and based in fact.

And for those of you who are building your new vocabulary of technical words, please find a glossary to help with this at the end of this book as well as a list of helpful videos that I've created over the past years to walk through some tasks that many authors struggle with.

Use the lines below to collect your thoughts on what you have learned so far:

_____

_____

_____

_____

Read glossary (vocab) + watch videos at the back of book.

_____

_____

_____

_____

_____

_____

_____

_____

_____

_____

_____

_____

_____

_____

_____

_____

1

THE GOALS OF THIS BOOK

For the purposes of this book we will describe the author platform as consisting of some or all of the following:

- A blog or website
- Twitter
- Facebook
- Google+
- Pinterest
- LinkedIn
- YouTube
- Instagram
- Goodreads and Library Thing
- Newsletter
- Amazon Author Page

YOU'LL NOTICE that I said "some or all." The purpose of developing a platform or on-line presence is to help you develop relationships with readers. You have to find your readers in the places where they hang out. They aren't necessarily where you want them to hang out!

FOR EXAMPLE, authors who write YA often have an audience that is made up of adults as well as teens. Where do teens hang out? Studies show that one of the popular places for teens these days is Instagram. If you are a YA author, do you have an Instagram account?

Also keep in mind that there is no "one-size-fits-all" platform for authors. Not only are different readers found in different places, you have to have a certain comfort level with the various social media you decide to join. If you feel like a dork, you probably look like a dork. Let me help you become familiar with the various parts of a platform and help you walk with confidence.

The last point that I'll make before we start talking about the various parts and pieces that make up an on-line presence is that I want you to see these parts and pieces as inter-connected. Maybe picture an old-fashioned wagon wheel. The spokes of the wheel connect the outside rim to the inside hub. In a similar fashion you want to make sure that every part of your on-line presence connects with every other part. I often suggest that your blog or website serves as the central hub with mention of every other place you can be 'found.' Likewise, your 'bio' or 'about me' statement other places will lead readers back to your blog/website. This will allow readers to connect the "Facebook you" with the "Twitter you" with the "Amazon you." More about this inter-connection as we move forward!

USE the lines below to collect your thoughts on what you have learned so far:

_____

my readers would use Facebook, instagram
pintrest

Connect all your online presences
blog or website - central hub

_____

_____

_____

_____

_____

_____

_____

_____

_____

_____

_____

_____

_____

_____

_____

2

WEBSITE OR BLOG

Let's start with the hub of your author platform—your website or blog. These words are often used interchangeably but can actually denote separate things. Let's define.

Usually the word "website" refers to a static site on the Internet containing information that isn't changed frequently. A programmer or web designer versed in coding usually makes the changes on a per-change or hourly basis. Many authors view websites as expensive, and they certainly can be.

In addition to the cost, static websites pose another problem. Because new and exciting information doesn't appear in a timely fashion, these sites don't attract the attention of Google and therefore often don't rank very well in a Google search.

Think of Google as a toddler with a new toy. Those of you who have had exposure to toddlers know the toy doesn't stay new long and before you know it, the toddler is on to other toys—always looking for something new and different – perhaps the box the toy came in. If the content on a website is rarely updated, Google won't pay much attention either.

Why should you care about this? In today's world of smart phones and Google searches, often the first response from a reader is to "Google" the author looking for more information. They will be looking for a website or blog or another online presence and most Google searchers don't venture beyond the first page or two of a search.

Because of this, as an author, you want to rank as high as possible during a Google search. Since most searches of authors are done by readers searching the author's name, if you have an uncommon name such as mine, ranking on Google is a slam-dunk. Search my name and you'll discover I own the first page of Google in a name-based search.

If you have a common surname like Smith or Jones, or share a name with a celebrity, you'll probably never be found on the first page of Google. A client of mine shares his name with a moderately successful country singer. That's a tough row to hoe. Ranking higher on Google than a famous person is difficult, but it is possible —as long as your name isn't Steve Jobs or Bill Gates.

Authors often ask "Why do we want to rank high on a Google search?" In fact, many readers will search for more information on Amazon before they head to Google, and many of your readers will come from word of mouth. To cover all bases, if a potential reader wants to find you using a Google search, make it easy for them to find you by ensuring you rank as high as possible.

Tech Hint: A lot of people tell me they "Google" themselves or search for themselves on Google all the time and they rank really well. Google is a responsive search engine. In other words, it learns. The more you perform a certain search, the better Google gets at finding what you want. If you Google yourself all the time, Google will get really good at finding you. Go to your local library and do the same search without signing in to your Google account. You will likely see a very different result from home. You likely don't rank as high as you think!

If you "Google" yourself, where do you find yourself? What page?

_____

_____

_____

_____

_____

LET'S RETURN to our discussion of websites versus blogs. If websites feature static content, blogs offer a constant stream of new information. To my mind, blogs offer a second benefit: an author can maintain a blog with minimal paid help in many cases. Most important, a blog's fresh content ensures it will rank higher in a Google search. (Remember the toddler example.)

BLOGS

DURING THE 1990S, a blog was known as a 'weblog,' indicating that it was something found on the Internet (the web) as a serial recording of information—a diary or log, if you will. Today, blogs are quite different. They are personalized and modified to display information in a variety of ways. But ultimately, a blog is still a serial collection of information.

In my experience, most blogs are designed by highly technical people with little understanding of the needs of authors. Even if you think your blog is 'the cat's pyjamas,' your needs and tastes will change over time – and especially once you start using your blog.

Please use the information below to make informed choices about your initial direction, or to modify the blog you've already developed. Whether you are a new or seasoned blogger, I hope that by the end of this section you will have a better sense of the components required for a successful author blog.

This brings me to an important point: regardless of your web designer's opinion, ultimately your blog must be easy to use and tailored to your needs. If you have a blog that is too complicated for your skill level, ask for help. Make sure that help is qualified and is used to working with authors. We are a niche group with unique needs.

There are many different platforms to blog on including Blogger, free WordPress (also known as WordPress.com) and self-hosted WordPress (also known as WordPress.org). Each platform has positive and negative aspects. We will be discussing the positive and the negative aspects below to help you make an informed decision.

As of this writing, a self-hosted WordPress blog costs no more than $100.00 a year. There are some additional startup costs. For example, how much you spend depends on the graphics selected for your blog. Remember regardless of what country you live in, the creation and maintenance of a blog/website is a business expense and as such can be declared on your tax filings. If you have questions about this, contact a local writer's group and enquire about an author friendly tax professional.

For a nominal charge, you may also register a domain for your free WordPress or Blogger account. Doing so allows use of your author name unless the domain has been registered by another writer with the same name. For example, I own the domain 'barb-drozdowich.com' and it is attached to my author site. Since many people who search for authors on Google will search the author's first and last name – having a domain that matches that search makes you easy to find.

―――――――――

ACCORDING to data from a website called Internet Live Stats (which tracks up to date stats of various sorts), there are over 1 **billion** websites online as of July 2017. That's about one website for every seven people in the world. That's a LOT, considering the fact that not every country in the world has a stable Internet connection. The take-away from this data is what used to be fairly uncommon and expensive, is now common and accessible by most.

Because I'm fond of stats, I like to bring numbers into the discussion of websites/blogs. Although it is difficult to pinpoint exactly how many active sites exist at any given moment, I've tried, where possible to get numbers directly from the platform. According to numbers current as of this writing, the following exists:

WordPress:
Market share – 58.8%
Active sites – 20,580,941
total websites – 311,682M

Blogger:
Market share – 2.5%
Active Sites – 798,125
total websites - 21,205M

Squarespace:
Market Share – 1%
Active Sites – 233, 753
total websites – 8,440M

Weebly:
Market share – .4%
Active sites – 509K
#total websites – 937K

WIX:
Market share – 1%
Active sites – 2.2M

#total websites – 100M

YOUR EYES ARE PROBABLY GLAZING over and you are trying to figure out why a beginner author needs this information. Ultimately, you don't, but I find it interesting to see the dramatic differences between the numbers. By far, WordPress runs the majority of websites. This popularity tells you a number of things:

1) People WAY smarter than you or me have done the research and have decided that WordPress is the best program to run their website/blog for a variety of reasons. Many of these people have designed sites for major companies.

2) Because of the popularity of WordPress, the available help and other support will be greater than for the other platforms

IN THE NEXT chapter we are going to start our discussion about the above programs and I will walk you through the process of deciding which you would like to run YOUR website.

USE the lines below to collect your thoughts on what you have learned so far:

_____

_____

_____

_____

_____

_____

_____

_____

_____

_____

_____

_____

_____

_____

_____

_____

_____

_____

_____

3

POPULAR BLOGGING PLATFORMS

In this chapter we will be covering the positives and negatives of the three most popular (by the percentage of users) platforms: Blogger, WordPress.com and self-hosted WordPress (WordPress.org). At the end of this chapter, I'll mention some of the less popular platforms to help you make an informed decision when choosing the platform for your website/blog.

Blogger

Blogger is a member of the Google family of products. Although on the surface Blogger is free, there can be costs to having a blog on Blogger. You can choose to register your domain for a nominal charge. I suggest you pay to register a first name/last name domain so that the readers who perform a Google Search for you using first name, last name will more easily find you. The other, more secondary reason to register a domain is purely aesthetics. The default URL that comes with a Blogger blog is in the format of: http://yourdomain.blogspot.com. People in the know will realize that you are running your business using a free platform and you haven't invested $10 or $15 in a custom domain. I am not trying to make a judgmental comment, just pointing out something that may make you the subject of comments. Judging people on superficial points isn't limited to kids in high school. It exists in the author world also.

To create a unique look for your Blogger blog, you can hire someone to create a theme or a look for your site or, at the very least, some graphics for a header. As will be mentioned several times in this book, the look of your blog should fit in with your branding. When I say branding, I'm referring to the overall look and feel of everything that makes up your presence. From book covers to other graphics, the color scheme, image choice and font choice should follow a pattern and fit with the genre you write in.

The Blogger platform is designed to be fairly straight-forward. I won't use the word "simple" or "easy" but compared to other platforms, Blogger is generally considered to require very little in terms of technical ability or outside help. Most users are able to work their way through the choices available or perhaps some YouTube tutorials and customize the overall look of their site.

Posting information to Blogger is straightforward. The posting window looks something like a word processing program. I believe if you can operate a word processing program, then posting to Blogger isn't much different. Adding various items to your sidebar (which we will learn more about soon) is also quickly achieved. Simply choose from a number of preset widgets (gadgets), add them in the order you want them to appear and then add some content.

Sounds good, right? It is, for many people. Complaints begin when users discover Blogger's limitations. These complaints range from:

• You have only 1 gigabyte to publish images - this may seem like a lot when you start out, but an image-rich blog can quickly start to use up space. Consider that a base line iPhone has at least16 giga-bytes of memory

- You are limited to 10 fixed pages. Again, this seems like a lot when you are first starting out, but it is a limitation that many object to.

I FEEL WordPress is more versatile but the average user finds Blogger straightforward and works well for them.

There is something you should bear in mind. Rumors abound that Google shuts down some blogs for no apparent reason. This happens without warning and all content is lost. Are blogs shut down for no reason? I don't think so. To remain in good standing you must adhere to Blogger's Terms of Use (http://www.google.com/intl/en/policies/terms/). If you are going to choose Blogger as the platform for your website, I would strongly encourage you to actually read the rules. It is heartbreaking when an author has their site shutdown for rule infringements. All that work can be wiped out in a heartbeat. The one rule that tends to catch up romance authors is the 'adult content' rule. I certainly can appreciate a partially naked man in a kilt on a book cover – but if that is what your book covers look like, make sure you blog is classified properly.

Even with the negatives, many people love Blogger's simplicity and would never use a different platform.

Free WordPress

Free WordPress, also known as WordPress.com, offers a simplified version of the self-hosted WordPress program. Again, there are positives and negatives to a free WordPress.com site.

Like Blogger, the posting window resembles a word processing program with similar formatting capabilities and a selection of preset widgets that can be placed on the sidebars. As mentioned above for the Blogger platform, I suggest spending a few dollars to register a custom domain. Remember, if people are going to try to find you using a Google search, they will typically search for you using your first and last name. A custom domain can produce that and look more professional at the same time.

WordPress, like Blogger, features a selection of preset themes or looks. You can choose from amongst these themes, some free and some available for a fee, many of which can be customized to one extent or another. You can hire a designer to help you or do the work yourself.

As with Blogger, the main complaint I hear about Word-Press.com blogs is that you are limited in functionality. Once you are confident and ready to spread your wings as the saying goes, you will find that this limitation chafes. You are limited to the WordPress.com supplied themes or looks for your blog, which may make matching the branding of your book covers to your site a bit of a challenge. You are restricted from e-commerce on free WordPress (unless you pay a fee), and your blog may show ads that you have no control over (unless you pay another fee). These issues may not matter to you. If you simply wish to publish posts and communicate with your readers, WordPress.com may do just fine.

Tech Hint: WordPress.com has been enforcing its rules lately and blogs have been shut down with little to no warning. According to the Terms of Service (TOS) found here (https://en.wordpress.com/tos/), you have to maintain your blog according to what some consider strict rules. Although more relevant to book bloggers, WordPress.com doesn't allow what it refers to as "Book Blog Tour" blogs. In other words, it wants blogs that have original content, not repetitive content that is common on blogs which host tours. I mention this here because I know that many authors enjoy helping out their fellow authors by promoting their books via tours. WordPress.com also has rules regarding what they call 'Adult content' and a racy romance cover has been known to be a problem. To ensure that you are operating your blog according to the TOS, make sure that you have a quick read of the above link. To encourage you, the TOS documents are very readable, not full of legalese.

Self-Hosted WordPress

As you may have guessed, I prefer the versatility and freedom of a self-hosted or paid WordPress blog. The posting window is almost the same as WordPress.com, resembling a word processing program. You can use one of the preset themes or hire a designer to make a customized theme or look for your site.

The sky is the limit for your blog's look—you are limited only by your imagination and budget. Custom graphics can be fairly expensive, but your blog is a key component of your author brand and deserves a distinctive look. Just as your books should have a consistent look, the theme should be carried through to your blog, as well as other parts of your author platform.

When I wrote the first version of this book, graphics and the price of graphics was a hot topic. Many authors I worked with complained about the cost of custom graphics. I typically spend more money, and put more emphasis on book cover graphics, while recognizing that all my graphics need to look professional. Unlike when I first wrote this book, there are other options available than was true several years ago. Look in the appendix of this book for more information on sites like Canva.com and Fiverr.com – both reasonable alternatives for the author with a tight budget. One other thing to keep in mind if you are looking to limit costs is to create a website/blog that doesn't require or depend on large graphics. In fact, what is 'in fashion' right now in terms of design, is sites that are very simple and straightforward.

A word of caution: a self-hosted WordPress blog requires more care and feeding than either of its two peers. You (or someone you hire) would be responsible for keeping all the parts of the blog up to date and operating well. It's somewhat like owning a car—you get to drive it, but you need to put gas in it and you need to change its oil and give it new tires periodically. If you don't know what you are doing, you either need to hire someone like me to help you, or watch some YouTube videos (or take a course) to learn. There is nothing more embarrassing than having your professional author site hacked and displaying Viagra ads rather than your book covers! As I will say several times throughout this book, if you are going to get some help, make sure the help is qualified. Your neighbor's son or daughter might be pretty handy with a computer, but does he or she have the specialized knowledge that pertains to authors?

Other Platforms

The other platforms that are often used by authors are Squarespace, Weebly, Tumblr, and WIX.

Squarespace powers around 8.4 million websites (233K of these are considered to be active). Compared to WordPress, which powers about 311 million active websites, it is small potatoes. Although you can try out Squarespace for free, it is a paid service with packages ranging at the time of this writing from $8.00 to $26.00 per month. You are currently limited to a small number of preset themes and the ability to customize these various looks to match your branding. Many people find Squarespace relatively easy to use and, like Blogger users, would use nothing else. Many industry experts see Squarespace as appropriate for an artist's site, or a visually oriented business site. It isn't considered to be an intuitive platform for blogging, however.

Weebly is a free "drag-and-drop" website builder. It claims to host about 509K active sites and has its supporters. Although it is frequently used for websites and e-commerce stores, it isn't commonly the choice of authors who need a blog. The blogging aspect of Weebly is considered to be awkward to use. Weebly is said to have a lot of themes or looks to choose from, but most industry experts agree coding ability is needed to accomplish any significant degree of customization. On the positives, the content of a Weebly site can be exported if you decide to change platforms later. Pricing as of this point ranges from $4.00/month to $20.00/month – similar in price to WIX, but that price doesn't include the domain registration. Many find it easy – it is very basic.

Tumblr is a very popular platform with claims of hosting 357.7 million websites as of July 2017. Tumblr is considered to be a social media and microblogging platform. The one concern that is repeatedly raised in Google searches about Tumblr is its X-rated content. Tumblr does not restrict the content posted by users or require users to rate their sites. Because of Tumblr's re-blogging functionality, there have been many complaints of copyright infringement by users. I have a Tumblr account and enjoy surfing through posts and finding things to read. I have, however, been frequently confronted by pictures that are not appropriate for my family's viewing. It could be that I need to choose my friends more wisely, but X-rated or R-rated sites do not need to have warning screens like Blogger has. Tumblr is often a secondary site of authors, but not usually their primary site for their author platform.

Lastly, WIX is said to host 2.2 million active websites. As of the writing of this book, prices range from $4.08 to $19.90 per month, with the most basic plan displaying WIX ads on the websites. It is considered to be a drag-and-drop website builder. I've used the WIX platform several times and have had the occasion to help friends with their sites. I don't find the WIX editor particularly intuitive. WIX was originally created for Flash websites, which we no long do as they aren't SEO-friendly and are often slow to load resulting in poor ranking in a Google search. For me, those two issues are a deal killer. WIX won't allow exports out of content if you change your mind and want to move to a different platform, once a theme is chosen, it can't be changed and many experts agree that the SEO properties are only good if you really know what you are doing technically. Combine that with the difficult-to-use editor, and I suggest that you look to a different platform to host your author blog.

So, are you any closer to deciding which platform is best for you? I hope you are leaning towards self-hosted WordPress! But I also hope that you take all this information under advisement and make a choice that is dependent on facts and not on which seems to be the easiest to use.

Other thoughts on websites

Once you decide on a platform, give thought to the look of your blog. This is where your branding comes into play. An author writing sweet romances shouldn't have a dark-colored blog with vampires framing the blog posts. A paranormal author, on the other hand, might prefer a darker design that incorporates the unusual creatures depicted in her books.

Avoid designing a black blog with white writing. They are difficult to read. Likewise, a glaring white blog with small sized stark black text is also hard on the eyes. The list of things to avoid is relatively short:

• Avoid black with white type or white with black type
• Limit the amount of stark white background
• Avoid anything flashing or blinking
• Avoid glaring colors like fuchsia, lime green or canary yellow (certainly acceptable as accent colors, but not in large blocks)
• Avoid landing pages that only contain graphics and no copy

I HOPE that this chapter has helped you with your understanding of the various blogging platforms. Regardless of your choice, in the next chapter we move on to cover the necessary components of your author website/blog.

Before we move on, however, take a few moments to collect your thoughts. Knowing what you know now - which direction are you leaning to for platforms? Use the lines on the next pages to begin to put together some thoughts:

4

WHAT SHOULD YOUR BLOG CONTAIN?

Most people know that their blog will contain blog posts—and this is the aspect of owning a blog that most people agonize over—but there's more to consider. All blogs contain posts, but they will also contain pages.

Tech Hint: A Post is part of the blog's content and appears in a serial fashion, usually organized by date. A page is considered to be a non-serial type of information. It is usually is found by clicking on a menu link. Theoretically, a blog can have an unlimited number of pages (except on Blogger where you are limited to 10) but in reality, the normal number of pages that a blog has is usually under 10.

Your blog should contain:

- An "About Me" page
- A "Book(s)" page and maybe a "Coming Soon" page
- A "Media" page

- An "Events" or "In The News" page
- A "Landing" page
- Blog posts
- Sidebar (1 or 2)

YOU NEED A SELECTION OF PAGES, such as listed above, to present information about you, your books and your activities in an organized fashion. We'll run through a list of potential pages, but keep in mind that your blog is **your blog**. It should reflect your author persona. Just because I say you need an About Me page, don't think you need to use that title. Feel free to call yours "All the Deets" if this fits your brand. Let your personality shine through.

About Me Page

You need an "About Me" page and one that avoids a cookie cutter approach. Create information about you in an interesting and compelling fashion. Selling books is all about relationships, and this is where new readers learn about you. Avoid posting a stilted formal biography or CV; write something that is more personable – more friendly – something that talks to your readers. Unless you write scholarly works, avoid talking about your post-graduate degrees and the subject of your dissertation. Your parents may delight in your academic achievements, but the average reader might find this pretentious.

If you don't already have a professional head shot, schedule an appointment with a photographer. Include the head shot on your About Me page. Readers are more likely to relate to a friendly looking photo of you – this will make you seem more real and approachable. I must admit I'm not fond of having my picture taken, but I do understand the necessity. I would suggest that you use the same photo of you on all your points of interaction. Examples of these points include your website/blog, social media connections, and even the back of your book (if you are including a photo).

Use the lines below to rough out an About statement:

_____

_____

_____

_____

_____

_____

_____

_____

_____

_____

_____

Books Page

You need a page called "Book(s)" with a list of the book(s) you have published. For each book listed, include a cover graphic, a blurb, a link to an excerpt, possibly a link to a page of reviews and all the available buy-links. Each entry should be neatly divided from the next. If any of your books has won awards, feel free to add the award graphic and share a few words.

If you have written several books in a series, provide information on reading order, and hopefully a synopsis of the storyline. If a reader unknowingly begins with one of the books in the middle of the series, adding this information to your Books page will give a context for the entire series. Also consider including an FAQ section to help readers with questions about the various characters or storylines.

If you have a series of books with interconnected characters, provide some sort of graphic to help readers connect to your books. A family tree graphic, as an example, may serve the purpose. Ensure any graphic used will display well on the blog, or can be clicked and viewed in a larger size. Readers love background information!

I read historical romances that often contain 8 or 10 books in a series. It may take the author 4 or 5 years to complete the series. By the time I'm reading the last book, I need help remembering the characters in the first one—like many booklovers, I often read several different series at once. The author knows the characters and storylines, but I often have trouble remembering what happened in the first book once I've reached the eighth. Before picking up one of my favorite author's new releases, I often go to her website and refresh my memory. You can do the same for your books to help your readers.

Use the lines below to organize your thoughts about how you want your books displayed:

Coming Soon Page

Do you release books on a regular basis? If so, consider a "Coming Soon" section. If you're not comfortable creating a section that will change with release after release, simply put the latest book at the top of the "Books" page.

Media Page

The next page you will want to create is a "Media" page. Most people don't realize that book bloggers can be charged with copyright infringement in some countries for using long excerpts or other commonly used items as part of a posted review. Does this often happen? Of course not! But you want to be as helpful as possible in the promotion of your books. When building this page for authors I work with, I start the page with copy something like this:

"All information on this page can be freely used in the promotion of the author's works."

YOUR MEDIA PAGE should contain your author picture and several versions of your bio. I've heard people suggest that you should have short, medium and long bios. Personally, I think this is excessive, but you should have a two- or three-sentence bio as well as something a bit longer, say six or eight sentences. Again, unless you write scholarly-based non-fiction, an extensive bio is really not necessary, and can be off-putting to readers.

You should also include a high-resolution cover graphic of each book along with the blurb. Although this information is on your Book page, the Media page should contain a rougher setup that allows for ease of use by review sites. Links on this page are not embedded; they are written in full to allow easy copying and pasting by an interested blogger.

Each entry should have all the associated buy-links beside or directly below it. Remember, you should be as helpful as possible to the people interested in promoting your books.

Lastly, you will want to list all your social media contact points, not necessarily as embedded links, but in long form so that they can be copied and pasted.

Use the lines below to collect your thoughts on a Media Page:

_____

_____

_____

_____

_____

_____

_____

_____

_____

_____

Events Page and/or In the News Page

The next page that I suggest is either an "Events" page or an "In the News" page (or both). An Events page lists your current or upcoming appearances. Maybe you are having a book signing at the local bookstore, or are setting up a signing table at a book festival in the next city. Make it easy for your readers to find you at promotional venues.

An "In the News" page lists your recent interviews, book reviews with links and stops on your latest blog tour. You will build goodwill with a book blogger if you link to her site. Being notified of a link to her blog by a favorite author can make a book blogger's day! It's a great way to make friends. It is also important for Google to see you linking to other sites. Of course, like making friends in real life, we would hope that linking to a site would encourage reciprocation.

It's also important to publicize your successes. Do I suggest you link to every review? No, of course not. However, as I said, linking to another site is a way of making friends on-line. It is also a way of providing social proof. We can define 'social proof' simply as what others think. For authors, reviews are one form of social proof to readers.

Most of us receive our reviews from book bloggers or reviewers on Amazon or Goodreads. If a review is particularly complimentary and balanced, post a link to the review on your page and thank the blogger for the review. Should you comment on reviews found on Amazon or even Goodreads? No. These are potentially shark-infested waters! Amazon and Goodreads are public forums open to anyone wishing to comment. Simply thanking someone for reading your book demonstrates good manners; questioning the review's veracity can lead to trouble.

Keep your Events page current and up-to-date. Readers don't care if you were interviewed 5 years ago. They are interested in recent information. However, if you are well-published, you may list older reviews. Periodically check the posted links to ensure the blog that reviewed your book is still live. If the blog has been taken down, delete the link from your Events page but you can certainly keep the quote in place.

Do you need an Event/In the News Page:

_____

_____

_____

_____

_____

_____

_____

_____

_____

_____

_____

Landing Page or no Landing Page?

Should you have a "Landing" page? This is a question that I am often asked. What is a Landing page? If a reader enters the URL for your blog, this is the page where they will "land." It can be a static page that serves as a source of information or it can show blog posts.

In the past, it was common for sites to have a Flash intro for a Landing page with moving graphics and music. Keep in mind that many readers may visit your website while at work or even when they're home relaxing with family members. If your site opens with music blaring, your reader may not appreciate it.

Flash sites are attractive. However, they can negatively impact your Google ranking. A Flash intro to your site is pretty cool looking, but is ultimately just graphics. A key point here is that Google can't read pictures unless they have information added to them. Because of this, a landing page that contains a Flash into, or simply a large graphic is equivalent to a blank page to Google.

As I just mentioned, Google's search bots will only read text. If you have a Landing page featuring only your book cover and perhaps a caption of "Available on Amazon," the Google search engine will only read "Available on Amazon." Such generic copy won't help you win over fans. Imagine the same page with your cover graphic, the blurb for the book along with the title, a few choice quotes from reviews and some buy-links at the bottom of the page. That's helpful—and will be picked up nicely by Google.

Do you want a Landing page for your website? This is a difficult question to answer. I've seen quite a few badly designed and implemented Landing pages. If the Landing page serves as a sales page and draws the reader into your site to learn more about you and your books, then I certainly suggest having one. If yours is less than stellar, either get rid of it or fix the problems.

Do you want a Landing Page? Use the lines below to collect your thoughts and also perhaps list websites of fellow authors that you like:

_____

_____

_____

_____

_____

_____

_____

_____

_____

_____

_____

_____

_____

Blog Posts

Now that we've discussed the pages you should include on your blog, let's discuss the design of your blog page. Although we've just finished discussing a static Landing page, most author sites have the blog as the Landing page. This is the portion of your site where you share information about you and your thoughts in a diary or journal of posts. You want your personality to shine as you interact with readers.

There are two camps with regard to blogging. One camp insists you must blog four or five times a week. The second camp suggests blogging no more than twice weekly. I'm in camp number two. Frankly, if you are blogging five times a week, when do you write your books? In my experience, authors either take to blogging quickly or are dragged in kicking and screaming. I'm certain the difference between the two groups is conquering the dilemma of "What do I write?" There are good courses that teach blogging techniques. I have also written a book focusing solely on blogging. It's called *Blogging for Authors* and can be found at Amazon and other retailers.

For our purposes here, we'll focus on blog details, not the content of your posts.

Post Header

The area that is called the "Post Header" is the information at the top of the blog post and includes the blog title, date, author's name and comments. Let's talk about these one at a time.

1) Title of the Post

The title of your blog post should be meaningful, contain several keywords and be compelling at the same time. There have probably been several hundred thousand blog posts written about what makes a good blog title. Since there has been so much written on the topic, I'll leave it to others to cover this subject. I will, however, leave you with my favorite resource for creating a great headline or title - https://coschedule.com/headline-analyzer. Co-schedule is an awesome site with many different helpful tid-bits.

Head over to CoSchedule and play with the functions. Use the space below to collect your thoughts or summarize what you learned.

_____

_____

_____

_____

_____

_____

_____

_____

_____

_____

_____

_____

2) Dates

One of my pet peeves is the presence of dates. Dates are an accepted feature on all blog posts. But must you include them?

If you blog 15 times a year, or only when releasing a new book, remove the date field from the posts. There is nothing worse than finding the blog of your favorite author and realizing there hasn't been anything new added in months. Dated material may make the reader wonder if the author has died. Did she get a new URL, move the site and not leave a redirect notice?

If you don't update your material, you'll frustrate the reader. This is reason enough to remove the date field if you don't plan to blog with regularity.

There is a different standard for tech bloggers who need to supply timely information in today's fast-paced world. I don't believe the same standard applies to authors.

3) Author

The next common component of the blog header is the name of the person posting the article. It is more than that, actually. This is usually the username of the person signed in to the blog in order to create the post. People are used to seeing usernames that consist of a first initial and a last name. It is better to use your full first name and surname for your author name. You'll notice that I used the term author name, not just name. The **Author** field should be the same as your pen name or official author name. For example, if your friends call you Mike Smith, but your author name is Michael Smith, your name should show as Michael Smith on your blog. On WordPress blogs it is possible to display a user with your full first and last name. It is my recommendation that you use this when posting to your blog. Later, we'll discuss what Google sees when searching your blog – the author of a post is quite meaningful to Google.

4) Comments

Comments are another hot topic. Whether the point at which a reader accesses the ability to leave comments on your blog is at the beginning of your post or at the end, it should be obvious, and leaving comments should be easy to do. Let's talk about both of those two features.

There are probably several hundred different ways to control the look of comments, from fancy plugins to captcha, to the ability to leave cute smiley faces with the comment. In reality, experts tell us that on average only a small percentage of people who read our blog posts actually leave comments. Shouldn't we make it as easy as possible for these brave souls? Many Bloggers go to ridiculous lengths to supposedly avoid spam, that they create an unfriendly environment for their readers to share their thoughts.

Spam happens. It is fairly simple to ensure that spam is held in moderation or segregated into a spam folder. Most WordPress blogs (and other platforms) can be enabled with AKISMET or another anti-spam plugin and, once configured, these plugins do a decent job of dealing with spam without making readers go to great lengths simply to leave a comment. Whether the prompt to leave a comment is at the top or the bottom of your post, make it visible. Use a brighter color if necessary, and don't make people search for the comment field. Once people find the right spot to click on, don't make them log in. And for heaven sakes, don't make the reader enter those captcha letters. I've been known to give up without even trying when I'm faced with those blessed letters!

However you decide to combat spam, ensure that your method doesn't result in spam appearing to the readers visiting your blog. Not only is it not professional to let people read comments about Viagra on your blog, it is an indication that your blog isn't set up properly. Ask for help if you don't know how to put spam protection in place.

Body of the Blog Post

Let's talk about the body of the blog post. Make sure the background color, font style and font color are easy on the eyes. The blog post must be easy to read or viewers will leave early. As of the writing of this edition, it is quite fashionable to create blogs with tiny font in a medium gray or light brown color. I'm not a fan! When I design blogs, I usually increase the font size from the default to 14 or 16 points, depending on the actual font being used. I also make the font color black in most cases. This makes the copy easier to read and the site more reader-friendly.

People who read blogs have the attention span of a gnat. They don't really read; they scan. They hop, skip and jump their way through the first few paragraphs of a blog post that you slaved over. Do you need to pander to this?

YES.

THERE ARE strategies you can use to keep people's attention focused on your work. At the top of this list, you can create short paragraphs—no more than 4 or 5 sentences each. Divide up each paragraph with a sub-heading, or a short quote from the next paragraph, or a single line in a different size font. Allow people's eyes to take a break, and give them a reason to read further.

Take a few moments and head over to my blog and download the graphic of the ideal blog post. Collect your thoughts below:

_____

_____

_____

_____

_____

_____

_____

_____

_____

_____

_____

_____

_____

_____

_____

_____

_____

_____

THE AVERAGE BLOG post for an author should be in the range of 700 to 900 words. It can be a bit shorter or longer, but it shouldn't be equivalent to a chapter in your book. Blog readers will lose interest and wander away. There are a lot of blog posts that will tell you that the ideal blog posts is 2000+ words – as that is what Google likes. However, that is an analysis of marketing blog posts, not friendly communications with readers – which is what I suggest for authors.

A magazine format for blogs is very popular these days. This is the format that shows the first half dozen lines followed by a "Read More" prompt or button. I was actually reading a blog article about this format and they claimed that it made a blog look more organized. I don't disagree. Although I think this format belongs on many sites, I don't believe it belongs on an author's blog. I believe it encourages a reader to leave the post without clicking on the Read More button.

Does that happen on your blog? Your analytics will tell you if people are leaving before reading much. Google Analytics (http://www.google.ca/analytics/) will tell you the average time spent on your blog. If it is under a minute, you know that your readers aren't reading much.

Tech Help: If you don't have stats on your blog, I have videos that will walk you through the process of putting Google Analytics in place – see the Appendix at the end of this book.

I COVER the topic of creating the ideal blog post in more detail in my *Blogging for Authors* book. The intent of this book is get you started on your journey of learning – not to overwhelm you with too much information. Hence this second book.

Linking In/Linking Out

There are several other good strategies for keeping readers on your blog. The first one is to link (hyperlink) to another post on your blog. This gives readers something else OF YOURS to read.

Let's say your blog post discusses how excited you are about your new release. You can link back to the post where you revealed the cover for your book. Make sure that you have the link open in a new window so that the reader can easily navigate back to what they were reading in the first place.

Maybe your post is about your upcoming free days promotion and you are co-promoting with another author. Link to your buy-page on Amazon. Also link to the blog of your fellow promoter.

Not only is it friendly to link to other people's blogs, it is considered good for SEO. The rules for Google algorithms seem to change regularly; there is no guarantee that what puts you at the top of the rank today will help you tomorrow. However, practicing goodwill with other authors and bloggers can only benefit your career.

Regardless of the official reason, it's simply nice to link to other people's blogs. It's the online way to make friends, and marketing is all about relationship building. Let's say you are posting about your theories on how to take advantage of your free days on Amazon. Don't hesitate to link to the articles that you were reading during your research. Make sure that when the reader clicks on the link, that link opens in a new window.

Let's say you now have a compelling blog post of a good length. It's well-formatted, spell-checked and linked both to other posts published by you, and at least one post created by someone else.

What do you think makes a blog post friendly? Use the lines below to collect some thoughts and perhaps jot down blogs or blog posts with style you would like to emulate:

ARE YOU FINISHED?

No!

Signature

You need to sign your blog post, and make it easy for people to both follow you and find you on other social media platforms. Use a plugin for this or simply end your post with something like:

"Thanks for joining me today. I'd love to hear your thoughts on XYZ and I'd love it if you could use those little share buttons below to share this with your friends. I can also be found on Facebook * Twitter * LinkedIn * Google+ * Pinterest. Be sure to subscribe to my blog so you don't miss a post. Sign up for my newsletter over on the sidebar to the right, to be notified when my next book comes out."

I find a lot of readers of blog posts enjoy what they read, but wander away when they get to the end of the post. Give them instructions and they generally follow them. The second reason for a signature is that it creates an obvious ending for your post. I find that people just starting out in the blog world have trouble orienting to the format. By putting a signature at the bottom of your post, you create an obvious end and helps the newbies understand that what you were writing is now at a conclusion.

Use the lines below to rough out a possible signature for your blog:

_____

_____

_____

Sharing Buttons

We've already talked about making it easy for readers to comment on your blog; we also need to make it easy for them to share your blog posts with their on-line friends.

Share buttons can exist in one of three places: at the top of a post under the title, at the bottom of the post, or floating along the side. It is possible to install these buttons with a plugin (or on Blogger you can use the share buttons that Blogger supplies or put code in place for custom buttons). There are a large number of plugins on WordPress that perform this functionality.

I would suggest that you put share buttons at the top of your post as well as the bottom. They should be visible on your landing page as well as each post. Many people are like me – hesitant about leaving a comment. I read a lot of blogs and find myself nodding and smiling as I read along, but when I go to leave a comment, the only thing that I can think of typing is "Thanks for sharing." Frankly, I would much rather share the post with my friends. I have thousands of followers on Twitter and quite a few on Facebook. Isn't it more important that I share with my friends than find some-thing scintillating to say as a comment?

It's lovely to get comments. But it's more important to you, the author, that readers feel compelled to share your posts across their social media platforms. This heightens your visibility, makes Google take notice and can quickly lead to more book sales.

Which share buttons should you include? I suggest you include all of them—Facebook, Twitter, StumbleUpon, LinkedIn, Pinterest, Google+, Email, Digg and Reddit. I don't care if you don't have an account on some of these platforms. It isn't your job to determine how your readers share your information. It is your job to provide interesting content and to encourage sharing. It is their job to share in whatever fashion they are comfortable doing.

If you are still reluctant to include share buttons, consider that Google finds it very important how many times your posts are shared. To Google, sharing is an indication of quality content and influences search ranking. You want to rank on Google, don't you?

Blog Sidebars

Let's move on to the sidebars. Sidebars are the areas to one side (or both sides) of your posting area. This is where you provide information that connects you to your readers. Sidebars aren't like a closet in your hall where you stuff everything that doesn't fit anywhere else when company is coming. Sidebars should only contain necessary widgets and information. These widgets and pieces of information should appear in order of decreasing importance.

As an author, you want people to follow you, subscribe to your blog/newsletter as well as buy your books. Because of this, the widget that should be at the top of the sidebar is a "follow widget." Although it is possible to get individual icons for every social media platform and arrange them down the sidebar, doing so takes up valuable real estate. I suggest putting one widget in place that includes all icons in one spot. It's possible to find follow icons that match your branding in terms of style or color. Let your personality shine through.

Below the follow icons I would suggest adding links to purchase sites for your books. Put your book cover into an image widget (or image gadget if you are on Blogger) and hot link it to Amazon, Kobo, etc. Make sure that when clicked on, the link opens in a new window so that readers can easily find their way back to your blog.

This brings us to another issue. I do realize that it is possible to have your own store on your blog to sell copies of your books. This isn't something that I recommend for several reasons. First of all, many people aren't comfortable purchasing online from other than a large retailer because of the perceived security issues. Secondly, Amazon is where the vast majority of online purchases of books are made, and diverting sales to other sites can interfere with your search rankings on Amazon.

If your books are available at many locations, consider using a widget that allows you to enter multiple links. Link to every site where your book is available for sale, not just a small selection.

Below the book links, I would suggest a subscription widget that allows readers to have your posts delivered in email form. Email delivery is a more reliable method of getting your message across than hoping readers remember to visit your blog on the days when you usually post.

One of WordPress' own plugins is called Jetpack. It is actually a collection of plugins that offers a variety of functionality, including email subscription. This subscription plugin is perhaps the easiest to use to manage your WordPress blog subscriptions.

MailChimp (http://mailchimp.com), a mass email platform often used for newsletters, is highly rated and can also be used to deliver blog posts. I prefer using MailChimp over Jetpack because it can produce a branded delivery of your blog posts. Keep to your skill level, however, as both will do the job of getting your posts delivered to your audience.

The items mentioned above are all that is really needed on your sidebar. I'm sure some would disagree. For example, it is considered good manners to advertise blog tour companies you've used in the past. Most have cute badges that you can litter on your sidebars. Do you belong to any affiliations, like RWA chapters? Again, many will provide you with a badge to advertise your affiliation. Consider limiting the number of badges on your sidebar. As much as it is nice to advertise things, you want readers to focus on your book(s), not be distracted by too much information! There are other ways to make friends than to post badges and links on your sidebar.

What else can you put on your sidebar? The possibilities are endless. Here are a few ideas. I like the idea of placing a Pinterest Board widget to show off what you are pinning—especially if it is visually appealing! I also like seeing a Twitter stream widget. Keep in mind that if you are not active on Twitter, that will be revealed on your blog. You want to emphasize the positives and hide the negatives! For example if your new blog only has 5 hits a day, don't put a hit counter on your sidebar. If your blog has 1,000 hits a day, absolutely put a widget in a prominent spot! If you tweet once a month, don't use a Twitter stream widget. If you are active on Twitter, use a Twitter widget and encourage your followers to join you on Twitter.

Ultimately, it's your blog, but consider this analogy: Your blog is your storefront. It is often the first place readers will view your work. Present a professional image at all times.

Think about the stores you frequent. Do you enjoy digging through mismatched piles of merchandise at the local thrift store to locate what you want? Or do you prefer to easily find your next purchase? Some of us are bargain hunters and relish the hunt, but the majority of consumers will find an organized store more appealing.

I've heard some authors say, "I'm an artist. I can't worry about technical issues" or some version of that statement. But you can't afford to convey the image of an amateur; you are a professional author. Present a professional face to the world. Quite frankly, if you aren't capable of performing the tasks outlined in this book, hire someone to help you. This help doesn't need to be expensive and is a business related tax deduction. You might also check for appropriate courses at your local college. It's amazing how much a few hours of training or an on-line course can help.

Take advantage of the lines below to collect your thoughts on what you have learned in the chapter:

_____

_____

_____

_____

_____

_____

_____

_____

_____

_____

_____

_____

_____

_____

_____

_____

5

AUTOMATING, BACKING UP AND COPYRIGHTING YOUR BLOG POST

Automating

Before we talk about the various social media platforms, let's discuss automating delivery of your blog posts. You don't want to rely on people remembering which days you post, and you certainly don't want to rely on dumb luck for people to stumble on your blog posts. Ideally you want make it as easy as possible for readers to stay abreast of your latest thoughts, new releases and anything else you wish to post on your blog. The public should also be able to follow your posts in a fashion that is convenient to them.

It isn't up to you to decide how someone follows you. Individual readers will decide how they want the information delivered. Some readers prefer to subscribe to your RSS feed in a website or application reader such as Feedly. Others like to have posts delivered to their inbox. I'm a fan of the feed readers (I use Feedly to read blogs). I regularly read somewhere in the order of 500 blogs. Do I want that in my Inbox? Certainly not!

In addition to subscriptions and RSS feeds, blog posts may be disseminated to many platforms like Twitter, Facebook, Google+ or LinkedIn, all of which can be automated.

This automation can occur in many ways, from plugins on your blog (like Jetpack on WordPress), to services like Dlvr.it (my personal favorite). The list is virtually endless. Sign into the service (or install the plugin on your blog), enter your RSS feed, and then add each social media platform that you want your posts delivered to. Make sure that your posts go everywhere they can without any work on your part. The last thing you want to do after slaving over a blog post is to remember everywhere you are supposed to send it so that people can find it.

Backing Up

Many of us spend hours writing our blog posts. I know that some of the technical how-to posts I put on my business blog take me a long time to put together. Between getting the instructions just right and taking screenshots that fit the instructions, it is a labor of love!

You need to give some thought as to how you are going to back up the work on your site. Many authors that I talk to assume if they have a free site—WordPress.com or Blogger.com—the backups are done for them. That isn't really true. Combine that information with the fact that WordPress and Blogger can eliminate your site without warning if you break the rules, and you need to give some thought to how you are going to ensure that your work is not lost.

Believe it or not, there is a quick and dirty way of backing up both WordPress and Blogger blogs—take an export (on WP see Tools -> Export). An export of your blog is an XML file that contains all the bits and pieces of your site. It doesn't include the layout of the sidebars, but it's better than nothing. Take this file and put it on an external hard drive or a zip drive and you have some record of all your work for your site.

I used to sit every Saturday morning before breakfast and take an export of all 50+ sites that I'm responsible for and put them on an external hard drive. Some of these sites had other backup functionalities in place also. While I had breakfast, I would set Time Machine (I have a Mac) to back up all my computer files to an external hard drive. This was great—I never forgot and I always made sure that I had a backup at least once a week. Then one of my computer geek friends wisely said . . . what if your house burns down? Or the external hard drive is stolen during a break-in?

Hmmmm . . . I then started using cloud storage for my backups!

Whatever you do to back up your work, make sure that it is effective and it is done regularly. Send yourself a reminder, or arrange for an automated service. Blogs are somewhat vulnerable and it would be a shame if you had to start from scratch.

Copyrighting

It's important to make all attempts to safeguard your work on your blog. Although there are several methods to do this, I like using the service of My Free Copyright
(http://www.myfreecopyright.com/).

This service, as its name suggests, is free. Once you sign up for an account and confirm your choice, the site will start the process of backing up your content.

You will be provided with some code to put on your blog to identify the fact that your blog is protected.

Is this foolproof? Of course not! Dishonest people will always find a way to be dishonest. I think that you do, however, need to make an effort to let people know that your work is your work, whether you do this by using a service or by simply posting a copyright notification on your sidebar.

Tech Hint: Many authors and bloggers create a Google Alert for a unique sentence in each blog post, to help police content theft. You need to decide how much effort you are willing to put in to deter theft of your content, and figure out what method you are most comfortable using.

USE the lines below to collect your thoughts about what you have learned in this chapter:

_____

_____

_____

_____

_____

_____

_____

_____

_____

_____

_____

_____

_____

6

SOCIAL MEDIA: TWITTER

L et's move on to the various social media platforms. The list seems endless, doesn't it? Frankly, how can you possibly have time for all of them and also find time to write?

Marketing experts generally advise authors to maintain a presence on all major social media sites, but spend the majority of their time on the one or two that they are most comfortable using. The point that is generally overlooked by many experts is you need to have a presence on social media sites where your audience is. If you follow the advice of experts and choose by your comfort level, your audience may not be there and you may be talking to a virtual empty room. Experiment until you find the sites that you are the most comfortable on **and** where your audience is. In the sections below and in future chapters, we'll talk about the demographics of the audience of each platform. I talk about this subject frequently in my books and blog posts. Don't hesitate to head to my blog (http://bakerviewconsulting.com) for some cool graphic representations of the various audiences.

The social media that we will be discussing are:

- Twitter
- Facebook
- Google+
- Pinterest
- LinkedIn
- YouTube
- Instagram
- Goodreads
- Library Thing

Twitter

Let's start with Twitter. Does Twitter make you want to tear your hair out? People seem to either love or hate it. Some time ago I told a friend of mine, "There is no way in hell I'm EVER getting a Twitter account." I now have thousands of followers. As a book blogger, it took me a while to understand the importance of Twitter to my platform, but I did eventually figure it out. As an author of non-fiction, I was happy that I made the effort to join and build a following.

Demographics:

Who is using Twitter? What I find interesting about the people on Twitter is that they seem to span all ages. As of this writing, there are 1.3 billion accounts with about 320 million being active Twitter users. Additionally, 500 million people visit Twitter each month without logging in. The average account holder has 208 followers, but 391 million accounts have no followers at all – that will skew the averages. There are about 500 million Tweets sent every day, which works out to 6,000 tweets per second.

Although people of a wide variety of ages are represented on

Twitter, most younger users consider Twitter to be "old school." My teen wouldn't be caught dead on Twitter!

Decoding of Twitter terms:

• DM - Direct Message—a private tweet from one Twitter user to another
• Mention—a message the whole Twitter world can see, which is sent from one Twitter user to another using usernames with the @ symbol
• Followers—people who are following you
• Following—people you are following
• Lists—user-created groups of like-minded individuals
• Hashtag—any word or phrase preceded by the # symbol. When it is clicked on in live Twitter, you will see other tweets containing the same keyword or topic – in other words a hashtag serves as searchable.
• @—a symbol that immediately precedes a username in order to send that person a message or to 'mention them'
• Tweet—a message that has a maximum of 280 characters and can contain a combination of text, hashtags, links, photos and video.
• RT—a re-tweet. This happens when someone tweets one of your tweets to their followers.

Other Twitter Trivia:

• Follow a reasonable number of people a day. What's reasonable? It is generally suggested that you not follow more than 50-100 people each day. Following a huge number of people daily makes Twitter nervous and can result in your account being frozen. This is commonly called Twitter Jail.
• Twitter wants you to show that you have some valid content to offer, so it prevents you from following too many people without a

selection following you back. The numbers exist in a ratio and this ratio will kick in when you try to follow more than 5,000 people in total.

• Don't announce to the world that Twitter won't allow you to follow any more people, as that puts a newbie stamp clearly in the middle of your forehead. There are easy ways to remove people who are not following you back, and will allow you to get your ratios in order. Have a look at http://www.Manageflitter.com, http://JustUnfollow.com or another similar program.

You need to use Twitter as part of your branding. There are three aspects to the Twitter page to consider:

1. **Bio:** Twitter limits you to 160 characters. Make every word count. You may include two links. I suggest one to your blog and one to your Amazon Author page. Don't link to a specific book you've published—link to your Author page. Identify yourself with relevant hashtags as they make your bio searchable.

2. **Profile picture:** Although a Twitter photo is small, ensure yours is clear and professional. There is nothing worse than a blurry smear of color for your photo. Even if you aren't comfortable displaying your author photo (although that is what I suggest using), leaving the default egg in place is unacceptable. The egg stamps you as a newbie! The size of picture that is expected is 400 X 400 pixels.

3. **Graphic Header:** This is the space that can be seen at the top of your home screen. It is sized to hold a 1500 X 500 pixel graphic. Again, use graphics relevant to your brand. If you are handy with a simple graphics program like Logoist or a site like Canva, you can create a spread of your book covers combined with a few words from a recent review. Make sure you view the graphic after you put it in place to ensure it looks all right.

The main complaints I hear about Twitter are threefold:

1. The program moves too fast.
2. The messages are too short.
3. Twitter is full of spammy links.

I wholeheartedly agree with all three.

Can you truly have a meaningful conversation with someone in 280 characters? In truth, you can. Think of tweeting as texting with the whole world. That is, old-school texting—you know, on your flip phone. (My iPhone will let me type a huge message without objecting to the character count!) Anyone can join in on your conversation, and that's what makes it interesting!

Is Twitter full of spammy links? You bet! It shouldn't be, but currently is. As I'll say again, social media reflects real life interactions in real time. Conversations should be two-way or interactive —they shouldn't be a monologue and they shouldn't only involve some version of "buy my book."

If you were at a party, would you walk from person to person, handing out business cards with the comment, "Hi there. My name is XXX. Buy my book," then move to the next person and repeat? That isn't normal behavior in real life. Nor does it fit in with what we know about book-buying behavior. Remember, books are purchased based on a relationship. They are purchased after a conversation with a friend, or a reader reads/hears a review by a trusted source. Or a purchase is made because the reader enjoys a relationship with the author. We rarely buy a book based on a newspaper ad or a billboard ad. Even then, a purchase is only made if we've heard about the book elsewhere. The Shades of Grey series provides a good example. Someone may pick up one of the Shades of Grey books after seeing the movie or glimpsing one of those risqué posters.

So, what is happening with the "buy my book" links that are

sent out on Twitter? Most are ignored. Twitter should be a combination of real conversations accompanied by branded information and links. You can absolutely send people to your blog or your Amazon page, but you should include a larger amount of tweets about topics connected to your brand. I love reading romances and I love WordPress, so I post information about romance novels and WordPress hints on my stream. If you look at my Twitter stream you'll see quotes from books that I've read, quotes from reviews of my books, quotes from a survey of book bloggers that I did, and WordPress tips amongst other things. Those tweets serve as conversation starters. They are commonly retweeted and commented on, which allows me to chat back on topics I love, and that are part of my brand.

To recap, your Twitter stream should contain both content and promotion. Promo tweets contain links; content tweets do not. Provide significantly more content tweets. Look at your Twitter stream to understand what it says about you as an author and a brand.

By the way, I don't thank everyone who follows me. Yes, I try to interact as often as possible. I will retweet something interesting or timely from another stream, or comment on something to spark a conversation. But you'll find my stream is not full of "Thanks for the follow" tweets.

Is yours?

Now let's comment on Twitter's speed. The worldwide conversation moves impossibly fast, which is why I spend very little time on live Twitter. Remember, in the demographics above, I stated that there are approximately 6000 tweets sent per second on average. The number of tweets you see will depend on what is sent by people you follow, however, the more people you follow, the more tweets will appear on your stream.

At the time of writing this edition, I have just short of 18,000 followers on Twitter and my stream moves at migraine inducing speeds. To deal with that, I use Hootsuite to communicate. Hootsuite is a social media management tool. With Hootsuite, I can divide my live stream into sub-streams, such as mentions, DMs (direct messages) and RTs (retweets) and lists. Luckily, these sections move much slower, I can comment back to people who interact with me or share content that I'm interested in.

Hootsuite is also available as an app for your smart phone, so you can take it with you when you are out and about. The functionality that I like about Hootsuite is the notifications that it provides. When I'm working, I'm logged out of all social media to reduce distractions. I have my iPhone within hearing, though and whenever a notification comes through, I can glance quickly to see if it is something that I need to pay attention to or not. I find social media is much less overwhelming if I manage it, rather than it manages me.

There are many similar programs you can look into to manage Twitter (and all your other social media accounts) successfully. I've used several. Investigate them and see if you can find something you are comfortable with. What doesn't work for me could certainly be something that you find incredibly helpful.

To monitor and eliminate people who don't follow back or who are inactive, I use ManageFlitter. Again, there are other similar programs. Find one that you are comfortable with and use it.

Now that we've talked about the types of tweets, the speed of Twitter and texting to the world, let's talk about why you have a Twitter account in the first place. Twitter is one of the top four social media platforms in use today. Where it ranks depends on a given day's survey. Although the younger set (early teens) aren't generally on Twitter, a large number of your readers, especially book bloggers, have a Twitter account. Because of this, you need a presence even if you don't spend much time on live chats. There are many disagreements as to how large a presence you should maintain. I believe Twitter should have a significant position in your author platform for access with book bloggers, fellow authors and industry professionals if nothing else.

For optimum success on Twitter, collect followers from various walks of life. Although it may be more comfortable to chat with other authors, expand your horizons and connect with people unrelated to the publishing field. For example, I know an author with a large following of adoptive parents because she's an adoptive mother. Another author friend works as a social media manager and peppers her Twitter stream with useful technology tips. Use similar strategies to ensure your Twitter stream is well-rounded even as you target book bloggers, readers and other publishing professionals.

A lot of information in this chapter! Take a few moments to collect your thoughts and brainstorm on ideas to use on Twitter:

_____

_____

_____

_____

_____

_____

_____

_____

_____

_____

_____

7

SOCIAL MEDIA: FACEBOOK

Facebook is the second social media platform on which I suggest you need to create a viable author presence. You actually need two Facebook accounts - a personal account or profile and a business/author page - or what we used to call a "Fan page". Everyone who uses Facebook must have a personal account before they are allowed to open one or more business/author pages. I strongly urge you to open a page in your author name. We'll talk about the demographics of Facebook later in this chapter, but first some rules and best practices.

The question that often comes up is "Do I need to have an Author page?" My answer is yes, for two reasons.

1) A Facebook page can be seen without signing into Facebook and, as such, is visible to all—not just Facebook account holders. Google actually indexes Facebook pages – not the content, but the page, and as such, a Facebook page will show up on a Google search, but a personal profile will not.

2) A personal profile on Facebook is only allowed to have 5,000 friends. Although this may seem like a lot when you are first

starting out, the number can climb quickly. An Author page has no such limits on the number of likes. Essentially, if you limit yourself to a personal profile, you are indirectly saying that no more than 5,000 people will ever be interested in your book. I find that sad. As with Twitter, you can add your Facebook page to your Hootsuite. It can be convenient (and less overwhelming) to deal with all your social media in one location.

Tech Hint: The shortcut to Facebook's rules is https://www.facebook.com/terms. In my experience, the rules that need to be paid attention to are as follows: 1) Facebook requires your personal profile has to be your real name – not a pen name. (Facebook is making noise about being more tolerant of pen names, though.) 2) You need to be careful about using images that are overly suggestive or violent. Most people are clear about what nudity is, but suggestive is a subjective thing. The same about something that is overly violent. Although I've been part of workshops in the past that show illustrations of what Facebook would consider offensive, when I look at Facebook's community standards page, there are word descriptions, but no examples. If this is something that might concern you, I would suggest that you tread carefully.

NOTE: In previous editions of this book I told you that Facebook's rules prohibit making money from a personal profile. In other words, you can't post about your blog or your book on your personal profile – this information must be shared on your author page. While researching for this edition, I found that Facebook seems to have two versions of this page in place. One that has that rule and one without. Regardless of what is out there in terms of rules, I would suggest that you err on the side of caution and focus your promotional efforts primarily on your Author Page.

IT IS my experience that most people have a personal Facebook account/profile. They keep in touch with friends and family members; they trade pictures of kitties and puppies, and graphics with pithy statements. A well-designed Facebook Author page takes the interaction with readers and fans one step further by becoming a one-stop shop that also includes all your various contact points. Did you know fans can access your Goodreads, Twitter and Pinterest accounts or purchase your books from Amazon or other retailers right from your Facebook page? I have videos that help you set this up HERE.

(https://www.youtube.com/channel/UCSgVt36XlVAHWj5dkSdo Zyw)

Most people upload pictures from writer's conferences or book signings but neglect to feature their own book covers. Don't make this mistake. As the owner of a page, you can also create events and invite friends to attend, host a giveaway (familiarize yourself with Facebook's rules), post excerpts of your work and link to your book trailer on YouTube.

As I am fond of saying, a fully tricked-out Facebook Author page is a beautiful thing.

It seems like a great place to be, doesn't it? Even if you have already opened a Facebook Author page, did you realize that all of the above is possible? Facebook is more than cute kitty pictures and pithy statements!

Recently there has been a lot of misinformation floating around the Internet. Some say that Facebook is going to charge authors to have pages—wrong. Some say that Facebook is trying to cut off their ability to do business with readers—again, wrong. What Facebook is trying to do going forward is make it more like the Facebook that we knew when we first joined—or at least when I first joined. It wants to make it a place where you can chat with your peeps, and share information. It wants to minimize the flooding of people's timelines with promotional posts.

Facebook is restricting the widespread dissemination of promotional posts—those are the ones with links. Doesn't matter where the links lead to, but one would assume they are a link outside of Facebook to your blog, your buy page on Amazon, or the like. Fewer and fewer people who like your page will see those posts unless you pay to promote them. People cry foul—how dare Facebook force us to spend money!?

Why not see this as a challenge to your creativity? Do you have to have a link in your post? Can't your post be a graphic that informs without selling? People know that if they want to buy your book, they can most likely find it on Amazon. Why not take a quote from a recent review and create a graphic out of it on Canva or Pablo by Buffer or the like? Not only will more people likely see the graphic, but people like sharing graphics. The word will spread! Try thinking out of the box and let me know what you have found that you can do to interact with your readers.

Demographics:

Facebook has upwards of 2 billion account holders as of this writing and they generally add 500,000 new users every day. Because of that, the numbers of account holders increase roughly 15% year over year. Facebook tells us that 1.09 billion people log onto Facebook daily. The 25 to 34 year old age group accounts for 30% of all users and 76% of these users are female. Users generally spend about 20 minutes each day logged into Facebook. The younger set (teenagers and early 20s) wouldn't be caught dead on Facebook – as my teenager tells me, "Facebook is for old people"...

If you write for the younger set, your readers won't necessarily be on Facebook, but their parents and grandparents likely will be (aka the people who buy the books) and Facebook is a great place for networking with other authors. The number of author groups of various descriptions is simply astonishing!

Take a few moments and brainstorm some ideas, collect your thoughts and perhaps rough out the bio you want to use for Facebook:

_____

_____

_____

_____

_____

_____

_____

_____

_____

_____

_____

_____

_____

8

SOCIAL MEDIA: GOOGLE+

Google+ is a Google product that can positively affect your ranking and therefore cannot be ignored. Many say that Google+ was created to compete with Facebook. Regardless of why it was created, it is a force to be aware of. Google is the number one search engine in the world and, as such, you need a presence on Google+. Google+, like Facebook, has two types of accounts, personal accounts and business pages. Ultimately, there is reason to have both, but we will start our discussion with a personal G+ account.

So how do you have a presence on Google+? It's rather simple. Create an account and begin to follow people. If you have a Gmail account, you will likely already have a G+ presence – go to http://plus.google.com and see what comes up. Start by finding friends and adding them. Google will suggest friends to you when you log into your G+ account. They will also suggest friends to you when they send you notification emails informing you of a new follower.

Like Facebook, there is a limit of 5,000 on the number of people you can follow. Stay tuned for more - Google+ is a rapidly evolving platform.

78

BARB DROZDOWICH

Take care to completely fill out your Google+ profile page. Your profile is comprised of a number of boxes of information. Some I suggest you fill out in detail, others you can easily ignore. The box labelled "Story" is where I suggest you start filling in information. This box is made up of "Tagline" and "Introduction." The "Tagline" is used to summarize you in a few words. For example, I have "Teacher, Book Blogger, Author." The "Introduction" section is the place for your short bio.

I don't suggest filling out the "Gender" or "Birthday" sections; I do, however, fill in a work contact info or email address.

The last box that we will talk about is what I think is the most important section. This box is called "Sites." It has two sections —"Other Profiles" and "Contributor To." The "Other Profiles" section is where you list all your social media contact points. Not some of them—all of them. The "Contributor to" section will allow you to list the URLs of all the sites that you post to. Again, not just your blog—list the sites that you regularly guest post on, also. All this helps Google determine everywhere you are and will help it connect the dots, so to speak. Remember, we are thinking networking here. Allow Google to create a virtual map of where you are and allow it to connect the "Facebook you" to the "Blog you" to the "Pinterest you", etc.

In addition to the profile, upload a few pictures to fill out your page's look—your book covers perhaps. Use your official author picture as your main photograph. The size of the profile picture that shows is 250 X 250 pixels. Again, like Twitter and Facebook, if you are handy with simple graphics sites like Canva.com or Pablo by Buffer you can create and upload a header banner showing your books. This is a big area and wants a graphic that is 1080 X 608 pixels.

What do you do with Google+?

You can do lots of things! You can share posts—we'll call it "Google+ing" or "+1ing". You can either copy and paste a URL into the appropriate field on your Google+ page, or click on the little G+ share button on someone else's post.

You can also start or join a "Community." A Community is a group of like-minded people. A Community can be created for any reason and people can be invited to join. Just like on open Google+, posts can be shared, but I like to think these posts will get more notice if you share a post designed for people in a specific Community. For example, I belong to a Book Blogger Community and everyone is a book blogger. I often find a post in that Community that leads me to a new book to read, suggested by one of my fellow book bloggers.

Are you wondering if Google+ is worth the effort? I think it is. I've read several studies that indicate people are more likely to find you on a Google search if you are included as one of their friends. I also read an interview with one of the top engineers at Google. He explained that the changes in Google search algorithms taking place (and making the news) are happening so that the searches will be more relevant to you, the searcher. Google is using a number of criteria, but they are making the assumption that anyone you are friends with on Google+ is your friend. Google assumes you'll find information from your friends more relevant— hence those friends appear more often in your searches.

Google is intuitive; it personalizes searches. It combines and analyzes a host of criteria in the hopes of helping you find what you are searching for. It is a good assumption that our friends would have the most relevant information for us.

What conclusion should you draw? You need a presence on Google+ as part of your author platform. Encourage your friends to Google+ your blog posts to help you rise in the search rankings.

Take a few moments to collect your thoughts about what you have learned. Rough out your ideas for a bio and content.

9

SOCIAL MEDIA: PINTEREST & LINKEDIN

Pinterest

As of this writing, Pinterest is one of the top four social media platforms. Some time ago, I opened an account, wandered through the stunningly beautiful photo selections and came to the conclusion that Pinterest had the potential to be a huge time-waster. Time I didn't have! With that thought, I quickly walked away from my brand-new account and went back to work.

For various reasons, I gradually came around to integrating Pinterest into my on-line presence and many of those reasons have to do with what to make for dinner and have very little to do with books! As we have discussed previously, a picture is worth a thousand words as the saying goes. Many Pinners (as Pinterest account holders are called) are attracted to the pictures of where to travel, how to keep kids busy with crafts and what to make for dinner and like many spend quite some time wandering around Pinterest. They spend time wandering from one board, one pin to another.

In my mind, there is nothing as visually stimulating as book covers. They brand a book, tell a story, and beckon to readers. I'm sure you've had the opportunity to wander up and down the aisles of a bookstore, enticed by cover art. You just know from the cover if it speaks to you.

It's no secret people respond faster to images than words. As an author, what better way to encourage interest in your books or book trailers than to show them?

Like other social media platforms, Pinterest allows you to create a free account, follow friends and allows friends to follow back. Pinterest has boards similar to a corkboard. The boards have names or titles and descriptions and hold "pinned" images with a small amount of text. You can pin an image or a video found somewhere on the internet (including your own blog) or upload an image from your computer. The image can have a title, description and a link. When the image is clicked on, the link can take the reader to your blog or your buy page on Amazon.

More importantly, your message is amplified when another pinner re-pins your book cover or other graphic to her board. When re-pinned, the graphic carries the link; if someone clicks on it, they will arrive at your blog or Amazon buy page. In addition to "re-pinning", people can "like" or "comment" on pictures. Isn't it gratifying that someone could find a cover of your book and comment, "Loved it"?

Let's briefly talk about the demographics of who is on Pinterest. As of this writing Pinterest is approaching 200 million account holders. In North America, the majority of Pinners are female, well educated and have money to spend. Each visit to Pinterest is on average 75 minutes! That's a huge amount of time on a social media platform. In Europe, the majority of the Pinners are male, but they are also well educated and have money to spend.

Do I still think Pinterest is a huge time-waster? For the average person—yes. However, it is a powerful tool to show off your book covers and book trailers and to communicate your brand to new and old readers alike. And this is done essentially without words; just pictures.

Take a few moments to collect your thoughts about what you've learned about Pinterest. Create a bio, give some thought as to what content you can share below:

_____

_____

_____

_____

_____

_____

_____

_____

_____

_____

_____

_____

_____

_____

LinkedIn

Many professionals consider LinkedIn to be the best networking site available. Amongst the author community the reaction is mixed. LinkedIn allows you to create a free account with a profile, list your resume, as well as various contact points, work history and a profile picture. You can connect with people from many walks of life and join groups to discuss topics of interest.

LinkedIn is a popular social networking site amongst professionals. Leads are found, and headhunters scour the entries for potential new employees for clients. If you are not a professional, and the only reason you are on LinkedIn is to network as an author, make sure your information is writing-related. If you're also using LinkedIn for your day job but are hoping to network as an author, make sure you list your writing credentials in addition to the information about your professional life. I am frequently approached by people on LinkedIn wanting to connect, but if I can see no points of commonality; i.e., if they aren't writers, I generally decline the request to connect.

I will caution that I find many of the groups are the source of "buy my book" messages that fill my inbox, and some of the "helpful information" is questionable at best. There is some validity to joining groups for networking, if nothing else. What I find most important is you can share your blog posts to your activity profile on LinkedIn—yet another place people can keep track of what's going on with your blog.

From informal discussions I've had with authors, many of the authors who find LinkedIn helpful are nonfiction authors. This doesn't mean fiction authors aren't successful on the site; it may depend on your genre. For example, literary novelists may have better success networking with other professionals than, let's say, a children's author.

Business professionals around the world use and recommend LinkedIn for a variety of reasons. It is a go-to site for recruiters and job seekers. I have talked to editors, publishers and agents; many believe LinkedIn to be a valuable resource for the publishing industry.

Set up an account, share your blog posts to your activity profile and see what you think of LinkedIn's potential for your career.

Do you below on LinkedIn? Do you feel you will have an audience there? Use the space below to collect your thoughts:

_____

_____

_____

_____

_____

_____

_____

_____

_____

_____

_____

_____

_____

10

SOCIAL MEDIA: YOUTUBE AND INSTAGRAM

YouTube

YouTube is the social media platform that everyone knows about, but no-one pays much attention to as a marketing device. Sure, users look up videos on funny car crashes or redneck water slides or the latest music videos. But authors rarely think to include it in their repertoire of accounts to market their books.

Depending on which survey you read, YouTube ranks anywhere from #2 to #10 in the Top 10 social media sites. In addition, YouTube is owned by Google. Just as you give a nod to G+, you need to tie your blog to your YouTube channel to augment your Google rank.

You can showcase your book trailer video or videos of live readings, etc on YouTube to increase readership. I must admit, when book trailer videos first appeared on the scene, I didn't see the point. Really, what do you do with them? The picture started to come together when I realized the potential. Your trailer can be added to your blog, become part of a promotion post, or added to your Author Central page on Amazon. Create a channel on YouTube for your book trailers, and people can subscribe to your channel. For cross-promotion purposes, you can also add your friend's book trailers to your playlists. This will increase traffic and exposure.

Think of YouTube as yet another opportunity to build your author brand and network.

Use the lines below to collect your thoughts about how useful YouTube will be to you:

_____

_____

_____

_____

_____

_____

_____

_____

_____

_____

_____

Instagram

Instagram is the new kid on the social media block. I must admit, I resisted this new site for quite a while, but finally caved and created a free account. I've been enjoying exploring this site and playing with its functionality.

What is Instagram? Wikipedia describes Instagram as *"an online mobile photo-sharing, video-sharing and social networking service that enables its users to take pictures and videos, share them on a variety of social networking platforms, such as Facebook, Twitter, Tumblr and Flickr."*

Instagram was created in late 2010 and had over 300 million active users as of December 2014. It was bought by Facebook in early 2012. It is considered to be one of the social media platforms favored by younger users although you will find users of any age on Instagram.

Instagram is primarily a mobile-based social media site. Although you can view an Instagram account on a laptop or desktop, the photos or videos must come from a mobile device through the app. Because of this, it isn't available to those of you who haven't taken the leap to mobile.

Since it is one of the places that younger readers can be found, if you specialize in fiction for the younger set, I suggest that you experiment with this new social medium. Even if your audience is older, I think that Instagram is fun and worth the time to explore as a way of sharing with your friends and fans.

There are several apps that are handy for creating graphics to share on Instagram. Have a look at Canva.com, Pablo by Buffer or Layout to help you create eye-catching graphics and videos!

Use the space below to collect your thoughts about using Instagram as part of your on-line presence:

_____

_____

_____

_____

_____

_____

_____

_____

_____

_____

_____

_____

_____

_____

11

SOCIAL MEDIA: GOODREADS AND LIBRARYTHING

G oodreads and LibraryThing are the two significant sites for bookish people to share their love of reading. Of these two sites, Goodreads is owned by Amazon and is the more popular of the two for readers (as apposed to book collectors.) There used to be a third site – Shelfari – but it has been absorbed into the Goodreads site.

In generalities, Goodreads and LibraryThing are websites that offer you a free account, allow you to list your books, comment on them and create a widget that shows your book collection on the sidebar of your blog. If you are a published author, you receive a variety of special privileges that will help you establish your community. Of the two, Goodreads should become an important building block of your author platform as it is generally accepted to be the most popular with readers.

We'll talk about the platforms in turn as they have their own positives and negatives.

Goodreads

What is Goodreads? To quote directly from their site:

"GOODREADS IS the largest site for readers and book recommendations in the world. We have more than 55,000,000 members who have added more than 1,500,000,000 books to their shelves. A home for casual readers and bona-fide bookworms alike, Goodreads users recommend books, share what they are reading with others, keep track of what they've read and would like to read, find their next favorite book, form book clubs and much more. Goodreads was launched in January 2007."

WHAT I REALLY LIKE ABOUT Goodreads is summed up in their reason for creating the site:

"Every once in a while you run into a friend who tells you about "this great new book I'm reading." And suddenly you're excited to read it. It's that kind of excitement that Goodreads is all about."

Here are some of the benefits of Goodreads:

• Personalized bookshelves with reader review and recommendation abilities
• Ability to join a large selection of groups catering to every reading taste
• Chance to become friends with or followers of favorite authors
• Opportunity to chat with readers around the globe
• Opportunity to vote on Goodreads' lists for such things as favorite books of the year
• The interactive capabilities are virtually endless.

I₉ TERMS of your author platform or on-line presence, Goodreads provides many opportunities to connect with potential readers and reviewers. Unlike Facebook or Twitter, Goodreads caters to active readers. If possible, join before your book is published and begin making friends. When your book is published, some of your friends may become your first reviewers. If you're still writing your book, start "friending" people now. You may have several hundred or even several thousand readers to announce the release to once your book goes live.

Join a group that discusses the genre you write and chat about books and authors. This is yet another way to network.

Goodreads allows special capabilities for authors. Once your book has been published (and in some cases before the book's release) an author can apply for author status. This opens up a whole selection of special privileges.

• Any account holder can have 5,000 friends, but authors can acquire followers and the number of followers is unlimited.

• Authors can add the RSS feed from their blog and followers will be notified when you publish a new post.

• Authors can share book excerpts and other works. They can offer free downloads to encourage new-to-them readers to try out their writing style.

• Authors can publicize upcoming public events such as signings or other appearances, or create events tied to book sale days or blog tours.

• Authors can post book trailers or other videos to share with readers.

• An author can even create a specialized widget to share her book's reviews on her blog from Goodreads.

Of the reader sites, I find Goodreads to be the most user friendly for authors. I'm sure that you'll hear complaints about maneuvering around the Goodreads website. I agree that the site could be easier to navigate, but with practice you, too, can feel more comfortable navigating Goodreads. In fact, I feel so strongly about Goodreads that I wrote a book entirely focused on Goodreads, and I've also created a free course to teach authors now to navigate the site as well as use it to network with readers.

Use the lines below to create a bio to use on Goodreads and collect your thought about this social site:

_____

_____

_____

_____

_____

_____

_____

_____

_____

_____

LibraryThing

LibraryThing offers many of the same functions as Goodreads. It allows readers to create a free account, list their books, review and comment on books, as well as several other functions common to the other two sites.

There are several things that set it apart, however. LibraryThing has two levels of service. For free, it allows a reader to catalogue or list up to 200 books. The paid service, currently $10/year or $25 for a lifetime, allows additional listings and additional functionalities.

Originally I signed up for an account because, at the time, it was the only place where I could create a widget for the sidebar of my book blog to display the books I was reading. Over time, this functionality became available from Goodreads also. I gravitated away from LibraryThing quickly as I don't find the user interface intuitive or particularly user-friendly.

However, the site was developed with the serious book collector in mind and offers two main features that set it apart from Goodreads. First of all, it has a very unique cataloging ability. Readers can list their books by entering the ISBN or by searching via author or title (as you can on the other sites), but only Library-Thing has access to over 700 bibliographic databases from which to draw data. This results in collectible and out-of-print books coming up on searches. Secondly, LibraryThing features an early reviewer program. This program allows some publishing houses to offer ARCs to lucky readers. If you belong to the program as a reader, you receive a monthly email notification of books you may request to receive pre-publication. A limited number of books are offered and competition by readers is fierce.

LibraryThing is proud of the literary environment it fosters. To quote from their help pages:

> *"LibraryThing is a place to connect with readers, not a place to advertise."* The Terms of Service state, *"Do not use LibraryThing as*

an advertising medium. Egregious commercial solicitation is forbidden.
No matter how great your novel, this does apply to authors."

AUTHORS CAN INTERACT and promote their books in designated areas, but spamming promotion is strictly forbidden.

Many people comment that the difference between Library-Thing and Goodreads is that fans of LibraryThing are focused on cataloging their book collections, while fans of Goodreads are interested in finding their next book to read.

Use the space below to collect your thoughts about what you've learned in this chapter:

_____

_____

_____

_____

_____

_____

_____

_____

12

NEWSLETTER

M any experts as well as many authors will say a newsletter is a critical component of a successful author platform or online presence. If the idea of sending out a witty newsletter once a month scares the pants off you, don't worry. Your job right now is to gather the names and email addresses of interested people so that, if in fact you work up the nerve to send out a newsletter, you have people waiting to receive it.

There are several methods to sending out a newsletter. I recommend a professional email service such as MailChimp. Although many feel that sending out mass mail through your email account is acceptable, studies show a significant amount will, in fact, end up in spam folders. Frankly, it also isn't very professional looking. When sending out communication to readers in the form of a newsletter, there are legalities that need to be followed. People need to be able to opt-off of your mailing list as well as several other things that are much easier to accomplish when using a service.

By using a professional service such as MailChimp or CampaignMonitor, etc. you are assured a much lower number of messages will end up in spam folders. My personal preference is MailChimp for two reasons: the sign-up form integrates nicely into

WordPress and it's free until you surpass 2,000 names on your mailing list. MailChimp also has the ability to deliver your blog posts if your subscribers so choose. In this manner, the program serves double duty. The professional services also help you maintain compliancy with the latest anti-spam rules that exist in most countries today.

When building your subscriber list, consider some sort of a freebie—a bonus chapter of your book or the chance to win an Amazon or Barnes & Noble gift card. Try a variety of tactics to encourage people to sign up to your list but, as one author recently advised, be clear to your reader what they are signing up to get. I have written 4 book box set covering the subject of mailing lists, newsletters and MailChimp and they can be purchased in a unit or as individual titles. If this is something you want more information on. See the details at the back of this book for more information.

Use the lines below to collect your thoughts about what you've learned in this chapter:

_____

_____

_____

_____

_____

_____

_____

_____

_____

_____

_____

_____

_____

_____

_____

_____

_____

_____

_____

_____

_____

_____

_____

_____

_____

_____

_____

_____

_____

_____

_____

_____

_____

_____

_____

_____

_____

_____

13

AMAZON AUTHOR PAGE

The last part of the author platform or on-line presence that I will talk about is often the most overlooked—the Amazon Author Central page. I think it is overlooked because it doesn't come into play until after the book is actually published. At that point, there is such a flurry of activity that the extras Amazon offers are simply forgotten—if, in fact, they were even known about in the first place. I am constantly amazed at the number of authors unaware of the marketing opportunities Amazon offers.

Once your book is live on Amazon, you have the opportunity to create an Author Central page. This page provides a large collection of information, but for now we will only focus on the information entered in the Profile section. Over time, you can become acquainted with the other features.

It is critical that you provide an Author Bio. I suggest that the bio be in the range of a paragraph. You can enter links to your blog in the text, but Amazon will prevent you from adding an actual hyperlink in your bio. The space that Amazon provides for readers to view your bio is limited by a 'Read More' prompt. As in other locations, many readers will wander away without clicking on that link. I'll remind you at the end of this section to view your Amazon page as a reader would so that you can make sure it looks all right.

To accompany your bio, Amazon allows you to upload a collection of pictures. Once uploaded, the pictures can be rearranged. Ensure that your professional author photo is the first one as this will be the image shown on your Amazon page beside your bio. A photo allows a reader to connect with you as a person, which surveys tell us increases the likelihood of a sale.

You also have the ability to customize your author page link (or direct URL). For example my author page can be found at: http://amazon.com/author/barbdrozdowich. If possible, I suggest that you use your author name. If your name is taken, use your first initial and surname or first name, last name and either the word 'author' or 'writer'.

Authors can enter their blog feed URL to their Author page. Once entered, a snapshot of a few of your recent blog posts will appear. When clicked on, the reader can be taken to your blog so that they can find out more about you and your work. Amazon seems to be always changing the display of this information to readers. Over the past few years, the display of an author's blog post have disappeared for periods of time, but they always seem to reappear.

Authors also have the ability to upload book trailers or other appropriate videos to their Amazon Author page. This area doesn't allow a connection to a YouTube video, but requires upload of a selection of file types. There's no question the ability to view a book trailer helps with the buying decision. Again, like blog posts, display of videos has also come and gone over the years, but I feel it is still a good idea to share this information whether Amazon displays it or not.

The last piece of information that you can enter is your Twitter handle. Once entered, a handful of your latest tweets will appear on your Author Central page.

When the Amazon Author page is viewed live, all this information is nicely combined with your list of published books. If you haven't already, wander over to Amazon.com and view the Author pages of some of your favorite authors to get a feel for what is available to you.

By the way, you aren't finished when you have completed your Amazon.com profile. Create an Amazon Author Central page for Amazon.de, Amazon.fr, and Amazon.co.uk. Currently there aren't any other Amazon Author pages available; we expect more to appear in the future, however, so stay tuned.

I've had a lot of authors wonder why they would go to the trouble of creating profiles for international Amazon sites, or they assume the Amazon U.S. Author Central pages feed to other outlets. They do not.

There are many reasons for creating multiple Amazon Author pages. First of all, many readers worldwide read in English. Secondly, it makes sense to provide as many pieces of information as possible to sway a buying decision in any venue where people may purchase your book(s). Although the other Author Centrals do not allow the entry of as much information as Amazon.com, the pages that are viewable look the same as Amazon.com.

Use the lines below to perhaps put together a bio to use on Amazon or collect your thoughts about what you've learned in this chapter:

_____

_____

_____

_____

_____

CONCLUSION

We have covered quite a few topics in the previous pages. While creating an author platform or on-line presence may initially seem intimidating, it is something that can be accomplished. Like any large, overwhelming job, do little bits at a time – don't attempt to do everything at once. Make a list, or simply follow through the chapters of this book and accomplish one thing at a time.

I hope the lessons you have learned in this book help you on your way. I have currently written 15 books to help authors and bloggers. I also offer 2 free books (not available anywhere else) to help with the details of putting together the various social media accounts. Simply follow the link on the next page to sign up and get some free help. I've also included blurbs and short excerpts from some of my other books to give you a glimpse into each one.

Don't hesitate to contact me with any questions you might have! My contact points are found below. Follow any of my blogs, wave at me on Twitter, or share a cute kitty or puppy picture with me on Facebook. My favorite thing in the world is chatting about books!

THANK you for reading *The Author's On-Line Presence.* I hope you enjoyed it. I, like all authors can benefit from reader reviews on retail sites like Amazon or Goodreads. If you enjoyed this book, please help other authors find this book by sharing a review on the platform on which you purchased a copy.

THANK you for your support of my books! I so appreciate it!

NOTES

YOUR HELPFUL HINTS ARE WAITING...

Interested in getting some helpful hints and some helpful videos to your inbox. As I'm sure you are aware, authors are encouraged to give away free book to encourage people to join their mailing lists.

My books are different - they solve a problem. Just because you picked up one of my books doesn't mean you want a free book on a completely different topic. Because of this, I offer subscribers to my mailing list, free help - usually in the form of blog posts or YouTube Videos. I let everyone know about new releases and offer money off of my online courses.

If this sounds like something you would be interested in, join me at: http://bakerviewconsulting.com/reader-list/

ABOUT THE AUTHOR

Social Media and Wordpress Consultant Barb Drozdowich has taught in colleges, universities and in the banking industry. More recently, she brings her 15+ years of teaching experience and a deep love of books to help authors develop the social media platform needed to succeed in today's fast evolving publishing world. She delights in taking technical subjects and making them understandable by the average person. She owns Bakerview Consulting and manages the popular blog, Sugarbeat's Books, where she talks about Romance novels.

She is the author of 15 books, over 45+ YouTube videos, an online Goodreads course and an online WordPress course, all focused on helping authors and bloggers. Barb lives in the mountains of British Columbia with her family.

Barb can be found on her Book Blog, Business Blog, Pinterest, Google+, Goodreads, and Youtube

As well as:

barbdrozdowich.com
barb@bakerviewconsulting.com

ALSO BY BARB DROZDOWICH

All my books start with a problem that needs a solution - with a group of authors letting me know about a subject that they don't understand. I take it, break it down and see if I can add some clarity.

The books I've written attack the subjects of:

1) Understanding the world of Book Bloggers and Book Reviewers

2) Understanding all the parts and pieces of an author's online presence at a beginner's level

3) Understand the world of book promotions

4) Understanding What to blog, How to blog and Why to blog for authors

5) Understand how to use Goodreads as a tool of networking and communication with readers

6) Understand mailing lists and newsletters

7) Understand how to self-publish a book

During a recent workshop I gave on self-publishing, I walked participants through an exercise to help them understand the power of e-readers as well as the limits of e-readers. I was talking about the fact that not all e-readers can make use of clickable links as not all are connected to the internet or have browser capabilities. We also talked about creating links that readers from a variety of countries can actually use - my example was around solely using an Amazon.com link. Suddenly the light went in my own head about all of the clickable links I put in my books. So...going forward I'm directing everyone to a page that contains information about all of my books and buy links that are associated with those books. The link is easy to type in manually or click on if you have the ability. It is: https://readerlinks.com/mybooks/733

Below find a short description of each of my books and don't hesitate to use the link above to find out more information in terms of formats available and places to purchase a copy.

The Authors Guide to Working with Book Bloggers

This book is the first book I wrote and is centered around information I received in a survey of book bloggers. This information has been updated through a second, more extensive survey. It is meant to serve as a primer for authors just entering the world of book bloggers or book reviewers. It helps explain the world of reviewers so that authors can walk confidently into that world and get some attention for a book.

More information: https://readerlinks.com/mybooks/733

The Author's Guide to Book Promotions

This book was also borne out of many discussions with authors. What is a book blog tour? What is a promotional newsletter? How do I determine which promotion company to use? I break down the language and explain this world in easy to understand English. This book also has large lists of book tour companies as well as book promotion companies which will help you start your search.

More information: https://readerlinks.com/mybooks/733

Blogging for Authors

Blogging is not dead as far as I'm concerned. It is alive and kicking! Blogging can be a very powerful way to communicate with readers. This book explains all aspects of blogging from what to say, to what platform to use, to how much it is going to cost.

More information: https://readerlinks.com/mybooks/733

An Author's Guide to Goodreads: How to Network with Millions of Readers

Goodreads seems to the site with so much power yet creates so much frustration in authors. I often describe this site as a rabbit's warren because of how difficult it is to navigate. This book will walk you through all aspects of how to effectively use Goodreads to communicate with readers. It also has a **Free course**

More information: https://readerlinks.com/mybooks/733

Top Advice for Authors Promoting Their Book and Book Blogger Survey

As I've mentioned previously, I've carried out several surveys of bloggers and written about the results. My first book, The Author's Guide to Working with Book Bloggers is the first book based on survey results. The two books pictured above are also based on survey results. The first one is simply the unfiltered collection of answers to the question: "If you could give an author one piece of advice about promoting their book, what would it be?" This book lists all 500+ responses. The second book is a full analysis of all 30+ questions. If you are interested in finding out real information about the book blogging/book reviewer world, these books will help.

More information: https://readerlinks.com/mybooks/733

The Complete Mailing List Toolkit

I like to say that this book covers mailing lists and newsletters from soup to nuts. It doesn't focus on one aspect of communicating with readers, it covers it all. Each section is available individually and this book also has a free course associated with it.

More information: https://readerlinks.com/mybooks/733

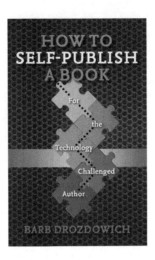

The Author's Guide to Self-Publishing For Canadians and How to Self-Publish a Book

Both of these books are quite similar in terms of content. I really wanted to write a book focused at self-publishing for my fellow Canadians - hence the first book. The second book is similar content but without the specific Canadian content. The references are applicable for writers in any country.

More information: https://readerlinks.com/mybooks/733

EXCERPT FROM BLOGGING FOR AUTHORS

What is Blogging?

AT ITS HEART, blogging is just another form of communication. In my mind there isn't a lot of difference between blogging and having a chat with some friends over a cup of coffee. You'll notice that I'm using the words "chat" or "conversation." When we're talking about blogging, I want you to keep the word "dialogue" in mind.

A blog is neither a billboard, nor a monologue. Blogging should be a dialogue.

Although I refer to the words "conversation" and "dialogue," your first response may be that no one talks on your blog, or that no one leaves comments for you to respond to. Times have changed.

The face of a conversation has changed in the electronic world. The person with whom we are chatting may not literally respond with words – they might respond with actions such as sharing your post with their friends on Facebook. They are doing the electronic equivalent of "Come over here and listen to this person." The electronic version is more along the lines of "This is great information; please go and read it." That's a response and in the big picture, that's a much more important response. Although I'm the first one to admit that comments are wonderful, such interaction is between two people. I have 16,000+ followers on Twitter. If I share on Twitter, it's pretty likely that more people than just myself will be part of the conversation. It's also pretty likely that a handful of my 16,000+ followers will join in, in their own way.

If you have a WordPress blog, one of the people you are "speaking" to might click on the Like button or in fact be so moved by what you have to say that they re-blog it.

And the conversation grows to include even more people.

The author's blog is a space that belongs to the author – unlike Facebook, Twitter or other social media. The author's blog is also searched and indexed by Google unlike the various social media (for the most part). This allows for your conversations to be searched for and found long after they take place. This isn't true of any material that you put on most social media. In fact, a post on your blog can be found years after it's created. The accepted shelf life of a Facebook post is considered to be between two and five hours and the shelf life of a Twitter post is 18 minutes. A LinkedIn post can have a shelf life of up to 24 hours in some cases.

An author's blog is the place where the author can share with their community; the place they can start or continue conversations and have dialogues. This is the place that the dialogue will grow a community of friends and supporters – people with like interests who will help spread the word about your book.

The content shared is based on the author's personality and interests and should be reflective of their branding. Yup – there's that nasty word – branding. We'll talk about branding – how straightforward it is – and how it's often blown out of proportion. We'll flesh out the topic of what to blog about, but first of all, we'll talk about why.

Why Do I Need to Blog?

THE QUESTION that comes up repeatedly during my discussions with authors – Why? Why do I need to blog? There are several answers to this question. At the top of the heap, blogging is a writing exercise, another opportunity to develop that writing muscle. The second reason is to communicate with your readers and develop a community.

We all figured out how to make friends in Kindergarten: "Hi, my name is Barb. Do you want to play with me?" As adults in the electronic world, the way to make friends is admittedly a bit more complicated, but not impossible. It goes something along the lines of, "Hi, my name is Barb and I write books. Let's explore interests we have in common and chat about stuff over a cup of virtual coffee."

The third reason, as I mentioned in the previous section, is to communicate and share with your community of readers in a fairly permanent way. Unlike the other parts of your platform, your blog posts can be searched and found months or years after they were first shared. So a post that attracted a new reader into having a virtual chat with you two years ago could easily be found today and have the same effect on a new reader.

Your blog is your public face to the world. In today's society if we want to find out more about a public figure, we "Google" them. Frankly, we expect all public figures including authors to have a website of some sort where we can find out more about them and their books. As we'll find out in the coming chapters, it's important to have a blog, but generally not necessary to have a website *and* a blog. A blog offers an author the ability to add fresh content on a regular basis to their site – something that Google LOVES!

Think of Google as a toddler. For those parents reading this, you realize that toddlers don't stay interested in anything for long. Even shiny, new toys are quickly abandoned for the box they came in. Google is similar. Google is attracted to new content. A blog that's posted to on a regular basis provides a steady stream of "shiny new toys" for the Google search engine. This helps a site rise up the ranks in a Google search. While it's true that the majority of your traffic will initially either come from your friends or be referral traffic from other social media, you want readers to be able to Google the genre they read and find your site in a search. We'll talk more about this in a future chapter.

One last comment for this section is about tone and language. As I've mentioned previously, I feel that your blog should be a conversation – a dialogue with your readers. A blog post that's a dialogue with your readers is typically casual in its language and tone, like a conversation between friends. It's meant to share information as you would over a cup of coffee or a glass of beer with your friends. If your blog post is more formal, it will sound like a dissertation or even a monologue. It may end up conveying information to an audience, but it typically won't turn your audience into a community. In short, your audience will react differently. Think about how you react when reading let's say a Wikipedia page. You're looking for information and you get it. Compare this to reading a chatty, personalized blog post. You'll have a different internal reaction.

I'll continue to remind you to keep the word "dialogue" in your mind as we go through this book. I find when you think of something as a dialogue, that is what you create.

To continue reading, pick up a copy of Blogging for Authors from all retailers: https://readerlinks.com/mybooks/733

What others think of this book:

Covering the basics of blogging, with a spin for authors, Barb tackles each topic effortlessly, effectively, and efficiently.

Since I am a few months into book blogging, I skipped to chapters containing answers to burning questions. All of my questions were answered. However, her teaching generated new questions, which I am sure her blog and other books will answer. - *The Literary Apothecary*

―――――――――

Blogging for Authors was an honest, in-depth look at what blogging entails and how to get the most from it. I knew a lot of the surface elements that goes into having a blog, but Barb Drozdowich in her book really made me think about more ways to utilize and maximize my blog. Also how to be smarter with analytics and the advantages of linking up an author blog with Amazon Author Central and Goodreads.

There were great links and some video links in the technical section at the end. Pretty much everything an author needs to blog and grow their blog is here. ~ *Brenda Lou*

―――――――――

I don't remember how I came across this book but it is BRILLIANT!

I love the idea of blogging but seem to always get stuck to what to write about, and also felt a little self-conscious about it. But this nook offers ideas, tips and systems that help you to find your own voice and present a professional and engaging presence.

This book has really helped and I find I keep coming back to it every so often. Great for authors of all levels looking to improve their blogging. ~ *Amazon reviewer*

EXCERPT FROM THE COMPLETE MAILING LIST TOOLKIT

Introduction

Welcome to *"The Complete Mailing List Toolkit,"* part of an ongoing series of author 'how-to' books, which is designed to help you navigate the technical issues of self-publishing. This box set specifically focuses on how to create optimized reader newsletters, how to grow your mailing list, how to ensure your newsletter arrives in inboxes and how to master email marketing services such as MailChimp.

I will use the word 'Communication' a lot in this box set. I feel to be successfully engaged with your audience, you must communicate with them, not simply bombard them with email and social media posts. Whereas many experts focus on simply gaining subscribers, I argue that this is too narrow of a focus.

Why this book?

Two reasons: 1) This book is well researched and pulls information from many different schools of thought and 2) I take a holistic view of communicating with readers.

Initially, my intention with this box set was to collect information from a wide variety of sources and condense it into a neat and easy to understand package for you. However, as I was researching, my opinion changed. I found that much of the information available online and in various webinars seemed to miss the boat in terms of accuracy, while others just seemed fixated on adding people to a mailing list like hoarders would add one more item to a collection. They weren't looking at their readers as individuals, nor were they treating them as such. I wanted to create something more "big picture-ish" (is that a word?) – that looks at all aspects and all facets, of communicating with readers using newsletters. Hence the box set. For authors who just want to attack one part of this puzzle, the books are available individually, but my wish is that they are all read together.

I come from a background of technical training and while I'm certainly comfortable with technology, I tend to be holistic in my view. I want to break subjects down into manageable sections, and I don't want to skip topics because they are difficult to explain. I feel that I haven't done my job unless I can explain complicated things and make them relevant to you. I'm holistic in terms of looking at one subject within a larger context.

In terms of communicating with readers, I don't focus on only one part of the puzzle in this box set. I want you to understand why I suggest using shorter subject lines for a newsletter. I want you to understand why entertaining readers, is as important as communicating with them. I want you to understand why it is necessary to use an Email Marketing System right from the get go to communicate with readers. I want you to understand how to work within the laws that govern your actions when you communicate with readers. I want to explain why the technical aspects that many overlook are really important to success in your endeavors.

Most importantly, I want you to understand that there isn't a one size fits all method of communication. The way you communicate with a teenager isn't the way you would communicate with a senior. The material that fans of romance are interested in is not likely to be the same as fans of horror. I want you to learn what your audience wants, not take the advice of an expert without thinking about it and without testing it out. I want you to learn to talk WITH your audience, not AT your audience. I want you to see your readers as more than a wallet.

Seems like I have a huge objective! We are going to break the subject of communicating with readers down into four books. In the first book we are going to address the topic of gathering the names of interested readers. We're going to view it as something other than hoarding.

Next we'll learn to use MailChimp really well. There are many Email Marketing Services, but MailChimp is the most popular with folks just starting out. If you have already chosen a different service, note that the lessons in this section are transferrable to other services.

In the third book we're going to talk about making sure that our newsletters actually end up in the inbox of our readers. This book will be fairly technical, but you'll have a good understanding of why best practices are what they are.

Finally, in the last book, we're going to talk about how to create really great content that is appropriate for our readers. We'll bring in some science, some psychology, and some good old-fashioned marketing to help you form a plan for going forward.

I guess it is too soon to say that I've really enjoyed writing these books... but I hope that you appreciate my efforts and learn to be better communicators with your readers!

Onward...

To continue reading, grab a copy of this book from all retailers
https://readerlinks.com/mybooks/733

What others are saying about this book:

Drozdowich gives the "why" and the "how" of MailChimp's

functions, and, even more helpful, shows what she uses or does not use (and why). This is so much better than the "you should" lists of some guides. ~ *Kay from Seattle*

Ms Drozdowich has an impressive portfolio of author related "how to ..." books and a well-deserved loyal following. With this latest offering, she provides help navigating this extremely important book marketing tool. ~ *James Minter*

It's comprehensive, it's detailed, it's accessible to read. It makes complex technicalities easy to understand. It's an extensive how-to set of books for those who want to build a mailing list and establish quality relationships with their readers through newsletters. ~ *Ana T*

GLOSSARY

Author Platform – also known as the on-line presence of an author – made up of a blog, website presences, newsletters and various social media accounts and is used to share information with readers and communicate with readers.

Badge – A badge is a graphic that's used to advertise a blog or website. Typically, it's small and square (250px X 250px) and reflects the branding of the website.

Blog – A blog is a type of website, which allows information to be added in a static fashion as well as a serial fashion. It can be run on a wide variety of platforms or programs.

Blog Feed/Feed – The Blog Feed, typically shortened to "Feed," is also known as RSS or RSS feed. A Blog feed or a RSS feed is a standard Internet technology that allows updates of your blog to be delivered to various places – other websites like Goodreads or into feedreaders like Feedly. In terms of format, it's typically your blog's URL followed by a slash and then the word 'feed' or http://yourdomain.com/feed. It is possible that your blog's feed is different.

Blogging Platform – A Blogging Platform is the program used to operate or run a blog. There are several – the most popular being WordPress, Blogger, and Tumblr.

Blog reader/Feed reader – A blog reader or feed reader is a program that gathers the RSS feeds from blogs and display them to be read. Typically, this program provides a pleasing reading format and a method of keeping track of what's been read as well as what hasn't.

Book Blogger – a person who has a blog whose main focus is books.

Branding – Branding is the combination of the look, feel, and tone that creates a unified and identifiable collection of information.

Domain – also known as a URL – is the address of a website. It's typically in the format of http://yourdomainname.com

First Name - Last Name URL or domain – This is a URL or domain address that is made up of a first name followed by a last name and then usually ending in '.com' An example is my URL – http://barbdrozdowich.com

Footer – The footer is the space at the very bottom of your website or blog. In some cases it can hold information in addition to a copyright statement.

Gravatar – a graphic that represents something – often a person. As an example, a gravatar is often seen beside any comment that a person makes on a blog post, Facebook or Twitter post.

Header – the Header is the part of a website at the top of the site and generally runs from side to side. It can also be used to refer to the top of a post – the area where the title is seen.

Hosting company – A Host or Hosting company is a business that has a collection of servers or big computers and sells space on those servers for people to run a blog or website. Examples would be Site Ground, GoDaddy or InMotion.

Hotlink – Hotlink is a common term to refer to a link that's attached to an image or some text in a website or blog. If a person clicks on that picture or text they are taken to another website. As an example, if a cover graphic of a book is 'hotlinked' to an Amazon buy link or URL, when it's clicked on, the direct buy page for that book on Amazon is opened.

Keyword(s) – A Keyword is an important word or collection of words used to describe something. Keywords for a book would be words like the genre, the city the book is centered in, or the time period. Keywords for an author often refer to works they use to describe themselves, their work and content for their platform communications.

Meme – a game or group activity played on blogs and/or social media. There's a common theme, a loose collection of rules and an identifying feature. For example, there's a blog meme called **Follow Friday** that bloggers can play. They create a blog post, post the unifying graphic and often comment on the weekly theme. They add their URL and other details into a Linky List and then go visiting other participants. Likewise, a Twitter meme called **#MondayBlogs** has bloggers post a tweet with an eye-catching title, a direct URL and the hashtag MondayBlogs to their Twitter stream. They then retweet and visit and read the tweets/posts of other participants.

Menu Bar – a Menu Bar is typically a line of clickable links either just under the header of a website/blog or in the header area of a website. The clickable links lead to other parts of the website or blog.

Plugin – a piece of code added to a blog to perform a function on that blog. An example of a Plugin is Akismet – it helps segregate spam into a specific folder. Sometimes a Plugin can also function as a **Widget**. In that case, it will have a function on the sidebar of a blog or website. An example of that would be an **Image Widget**.

Post (Posting) or blog post – A collection of words and pictures that are published and then visible on that blog. The word "Post" is frequently used to refer to an entry (often words and pictures) put on Facebook, Twitter, or other social media.

Re-Blog – to Re-blog is to copy and paste material from one blog post to another. It's either officially done by the 'Reblog' function available on several blogging platforms, or simply copy/paste. To avoid copyright issues, ensure proper attribution.

Search engine – A Search Engine is a very complicated computer program that searches a collection of websites to find entries for given words. An example is Google.

SEO – SEO stands for Search Engine Optimization. SEO is a collection of activities we perform on blogs/websites that make it easier for search engines to find and search them. These activities range from careful use of keywords, to linking to other blogs, to the addition of helpful information to pictures, among other examples.

Sidebar – The area on one or both sides of a website or blog. It contains content that's placed there often in the form of widgets or gadgets.

Social Proof – What others think of something. Examples of social proof are book reviews of a book, shares on Facebook or other social media of a blog post.

Tags – The word "Tag" or "Tags" has many meanings. Most commonly it refers to bits of HTML coding with specific meaning. The H1 tag stands for Heading 1 tag – meaning the highest level of heading. An "em" tag stands for italics and a "strong" tag stands for bold. Tags are said to be 'wrapped' around text. Tags have their own language of a sort where <h1> means start the h1 and </h1> means stop the h1. So, to wrap the text – <h1>The Title is Here</h1> will mark the phrase "The Title is Here" as the main title of a blog post.

Similarly, Here will make the word "Here" appear bold.

Theme – A collection of coding that controls the look and feel of a blog.

URL – The direct link or hyperlink to a post. It can be referred to as a Domain, but can also be used to show the exact link to a specific entry on a website.

Website – A site on the Internet

Widget – A collection of code used to perform a specific function (usually) on the sidebar of a website or blog. An example of a widget is an **Image Widget** that is used to hold a picture on the sidebar of a WordPress blog.

VIDEOS

Videos

WordPress Instruction

How to Customize your Dashboard and other Workspaces on WordPress:

https://www.youtube.com/watch?v=PdbevOSVS-I

How to Insert & Size Pictures in a WordPress Post or Page:

https://www.youtube.com/watch?v=MJZ9tLveX7s

Making Pictures Behave in WordPress Posts or Pages: https://www.youtube.com/watch?v=jgmKewZbtcw

How to Attach a Link to a Picture in a WordPress Post/Page:

https://www.youtube.com/watch?v=58IQZAlMrFU

How to Use Tiled Galleries in a WordPress Post:

https://www.youtube.com/watch?v=IHWXh3kKeho

How to use Different or Alternate Sources of Pictures for your WordPress Post or Page:
https://www.youtube.com/watch?v=pETRYZLr4vI

Formatting Text in a WordPress Post or Page:
https://www.youtube.com/watch?v=CGQuJsNq5Zs

How to Put HTML or iFrame code in a Widget in WordPress:
https://www.youtube.com/watch?v=AsHrrZawe9g

How to Embed a YouTube Video in a WordPress Post:
https://www.youtube.com/watch?v=Fhjoy6MzMvE

How to Insert a YouTube Video in a WordPress Post:
https://www.youtube.com/watch?v=Fhjoy6MzMvE

How to Edit Pictures Using the Editing Functions on WP:
https://www.youtube.com/watch?v=bCgx2oeEswQ

How to Create HTML Code to Put Follow Icons on the Sidebar in WP:
https://www.youtube.com/watch?v=dxqDti89gco

How to Add Google Analytics to a WordPress blog:

https://www.youtube.com/watch?v=Loiqu6ievQw

How to Embed Hyperlinks in a WordPress Post or Page:
https://www.youtube.com/watch?v=ptp34EU44Mc

How to Optimize your WordPress Post
https://www.youtube.com/watch?v=vJ8EfxK8eic

How to choose between WordPress.com and WordPress.org
https://www.youtube.com/watch?v=4NxrUQOuL6g

Videos About Amazon and Your Blog:
How to Add Amazon Affiliate Links to a Post/Page in WordPress:
https://www.youtube.com/watch?v=d3625R0yfJo

Why Use Amazon Affiliate Links on your Blog:
https://www.youtube.com/watch?v=J7n4p5c7VGs
Blogger Instruction:
How to Link Pictures on a Blogger Post or Page:
https://www.youtube.com/watch?v=eHxhDzbGnaQ&spfreload=10

Manipulating Images in Blogger Posts or Pages:
https://www.youtube.com/watch?v=BUZYooOC4sM

How to Put an Image on the Sidebar of a Blogger Blog:
https://www.youtube.com/watch?v=7Ywjvgo8wTM

How to Put HTML or iFrame code on the Sidebar of a Blogger Blog:
https://www.youtube.com/watch?v=jwtO-6-YXHM

How to Format Text in a Blogger Post:
https://www.youtube.com/watch?v=huNpD9-PKS0

How to Insert a YouTube Video in a Blogger Post:
https://www.youtube.com/watch?v=zXp-lI5B628

How to Put Code on the Sidebar of a Blogger Blog:
https://www.youtube.com/watch?v=jwtO-6-YXHM

How to Put an Image on the Sidebar of a Blogger Blog:
https://www.youtube.com/watch?v=yg7QAF6jIt0

How to Add Google Analytics to a Blogger Blog:
https://www.youtube.com/watch?v=Ific90gGJrg

Tech Tidbits for All Bloggers:
How to Put a Signature at the Bottom of a Blog Post:
https://www.youtube.com/watch?v=MAheCmM887s

The Cheater's Way of Creating HTML Using a Blog Post:
https://www.youtube.com/watch?v=c6jWVV9BWYQ

How to Create Export Files to Serve as Backup Files on WP and Blogger:

https://www.youtube.com/watch?v=E_Nl468dJCk

How to Display your Website/Blog on your Facebook Page

https://www.youtube.com/watch?v=-3AYGuxwI4k

How to Display your Pinterest page on your Facebook Page

https://www.youtube.com/watch?v=lsJaU-NoesM

How to add a YouTube video to your Facebook Page

https://www.youtube.com/watch?v=BzIbALjIYjo

How to display your YouTube Channel on your Facebook Page

https://www.youtube.com/watch?v=ZwtnA_961FQ

How to display a Twitter stream on your Facebook Page

https://www.youtube.com/watch?v=e4kvTpEy294

How to connect your Goodreads account to your Facebook Page

https://www.youtube.com/watch?v=Clwt4oIkzpI

How to create books easily using Vellum

https://www.youtube.com/watch?v=M2h7usWlHhg

How to use Canva to create graphics for social media posts

https://www.youtube.com/watch?v=KFpjj4BrwYg

How to load a Kindle ebook on to your Kindle device or App
https://www.youtube.com/watch?v=VPhfHawMn4A

I regularly add new videos to my YouTube channel. To keep up to date with additions, subscribe to my channel, here or subscribe to my blog here. (links also part of my author bio)

Made in the USA
Lexington, KY
28 September 2018